P9-CBS-618

The Curious Gardeners'
Six Elements of Garden Design

The Curious Gardeners'
Six Elements of Garden Design

GUY COOPER AND GORDON TAYLOR

Photographs by Clive Boursnell

headline

HOUSTON PUBLIC LIBRARY

R01242 91246

Text Copyright © 2002 Guy Cooper and Gordon Taylor
Photographs Copyright © 2002 Clive Boursnell except English Heritage/James Darwin 45; Marianne Majerus 178; National Trust Photographic Library 11, 56 below, 104, 137; Ushida-Findlay Partnership 92 (Katsuhisa Kida), 94-5 (James Harris); West Green House 130 below

The right of Guy Cooper and Gordon Taylor to be identified as the Authors of the Work has been asserted by them in accordance with the Copyright, Designs and Patents Act 1988.

First published in 2002
by HEADLINE BOOK PUBLISHING

By arrangement with the BBC

The BBC logo and the 'Curious Gardeners' logo are trade marks of the British Broadcasting Corporation and are used under licence

BBC logo © BBC 1996
'The Curious Gardeners' logo © BBC 2000

Guy Cooper and Gordon Taylor would be happy to hear from readers with their comments on the book at the following e-mail address:
g.taylor@clara.net

10 9 8 7 6 5 4 3 2 1

All rights reserved. No part of this publication may be reproduced, stored in a retrieval system, or transmitted, in any form or by any means without the prior written permission of the publisher, nor be otherwise circulated in any form of binding or cover other than that in which it is published and without a similar condition being imposed on the subsequent purchaser.

British Library Cataloguing in Publication Data

Cooper, Guy, 1934–
The curious gardeners' six elements of garden design
1. Gardens – Design
I. Title II. Taylor, Gordon, 1935–
712.6

ISBN 0 7553 1068 3

Designed by Andrew Barron @ Thextension
Edited by Serena Dilnot
Printed and bound in Great Britain by Butler & Tanner Ltd, Frome and London

HEADLINE BOOK PUBLISHING
A division of Hodder Headline
338 Euston Road
London NW1 3BH

Every effort has been made to fulfil requirements with regard to reproducing copyright material. The author and publisher will be glad to rectify any omissions at the earliest opportunity.

www.headline.co.uk
www.hodderheadline.com

Master view (previous spread) of grassed Claremont amphitheatre; design influences attributed perhaps to two Renaissance architects, either Bramante or Serlio.

ALSO BY GUY COOPER AND GORDON TAYLOR

ENGLISH HERB GARDENS

ENGLISH WATER GARDENS

PARADISE TRANSFORMED:
THE PRIVATE GARDEN FOR THE TWENTY-FIRST CENTURY

GARDENS OF OBSESSION:
ECCENTRIC AND EXTRAVAGANT VISIONS

GARDENS FOR THE FUTURE:
GESTURES AGAINST THE WILD

MIRRORS OF PARADISE:
THE GARDENS OF FERNANDO CARUNCHO

THE CURIOUS GARDENERS:
OBSESSION AND DIVERSITY IN 45 BRITISH GARDENS

A CLASSICAL GUARD (RIGHT) AS AN EYE-CATCHER AT THE END OF TWO DIFFERENT *ALLÉES* AT SISSINGHURST CASTLE.

THE UNDEPENDABLE RIVER SKELL (OVERLEAF) IS MOMENTARILY CONTROLLED BETWEEN THE RUINS OF FOUNTAINS ABBEY AND THE MIRRORED SURFACES OF THE MOON PONDS.

Acknowledgements

Second time around, it all seemed much more professional, or perhaps we were, up to a point, more certain and assured about what we knew and wanted in the new series.

There was almost an entirely new team at BBC Bristol, with Ian Pye, the executive director for all six episodes. He had also been the director of the first four minutes ever (the try-out pilot which will never be seen) of us on film, before we were transformed into the Curious Gardeners. But those four minutes must have encouraged Jane Root, Controller of BBC2, to commission the first series.

Ian was most ably assisted by Katie Lee on locations. And 'back at the Bristol ranch' production office, there was Anne Varley, Russell Jordan, Lotti Kierkegaard and Chris Mallet the editor.

The camera men were our good friend John Couzens, plus Robin Cox, Ian Young and Chris Goodyear. The sound men were Gordon Nightingale, another friend, who heard everything and diplomatically recorded only that which was necessary, John McCombie, Paul Hellard and Nick Reeks. The overall executive producer was Mark Hill, assisted by the ever-present Linda Griffiths.

Patricia White and Rebecca Price of Rogers, Coleridge and White continue to look after our money. Again, Heather Holden-Brown and Celia Kent encouraged us to write this book in record time, keeping just ahead of Clive Boursnell, who has been taking his wonderful photographs. Some of the gardens would not have been in this series without the kind help, depth of knowledge and inspiration of Jane Owen and Tim Richardson.

By the way, many, many thanks to all of the foregoing

With much gratitude to Charles Jencks

and for

the profound quotation in his London garden:

THE FUTURE IS BEHIND YOU

CONTENTS

Introduction **10**

time I 7

form 2 47

materials 3 7I

The Manor House,
Upton Grey, Hampshire **20**
Mount Stuart,
Isle of Bute, Scotland **24**
Sissinghurst Castle,
Cranbrook, Kent **30**
Levens Hall,
Kendal, Cumbria **34**
The Leonard Hotel,
Mayfair, London **38**
Maize Maze,
Crawley, West Sussex **40**
Witley Court,
Great Witley, Worcestershire **43**

Hawkstone Park,
Weston-Under-Redcastle,
Shropshire **50**
Hidcote Manor,
Chipping Campden,
Gloucestershire **54**
Claremont Landscape Gardens,
Esher, Surrey **58**
Shill House,
Alvescot, Oxfordshire **60**
National Botanic Garden of Wales,
Carmarthenshire, Wales **62**
The Lyceum,
Newport, Essex **65**
The Lexington,
City Road, City of London **68**

Hestercombe,
Taunton, Somerset **74**
St Catherine's College,
Oxford **80**
Three Gardens
by Tindale & Batstone
Cardiff and London **84**
Ultra Modern Garden,
Kennington, South London **88**
Flora's Garden,
Durngate, Northamptonshire **90**
Thatched Pool House,
Southern England **92**
Hackney Community College,
Shoreditch, East London **96**

water 4 99

sculpture 5 125

plants 6 157

Fountains Abbey and Studley Royal,
Ripon, North Yorkshire **102**
Shute House,
Shaftesbury, Dorset **106**
Somerset House,
The Strand, London **110**
Antony,
Torpoint, Cornwall **114**
Naturalistic Lake,
Storrington, West Sussex **118**
Floating Gardens,
Epping, Essex **122**

West Green House,
Hartley Wintney, Hampshire **128**
Silverstone Farm,
Norfolk **132**
Anglesey Abbey,
Lode, Cambridgeshire **136**
Trewyn Studio,
St Ives, Cornwall **140**
Half Acre,
Boscastle, Cornwall **144**
Garden in Mind,
Stanstead Park, Rowlands Castle,
West Sussex **146**
Gardens of Gaia,
Cranbrook, Kent **152**

Hadspen Garden and Nursery,
Castle Cary, Somerset **160**
Port Lympne,
Hythe, Kent **164**
Framed Planting,
Gosport, Hampshire **168**
Great Dixter,
Rye, East Sussex **170**
Jenningsbury Farm,
Hertfordshire **176**
Bury Court,
Farnham, Surrey **179**
The Beth Chatto Gardens,
Colchester, Essex **182**

Select Bibliography **186**
Index **190**

UPTON GREY WONDERFULLY
HEADY ROSES AND LILIES IN A
HAMPSHIRE PARTERRE (RIGHT);
1908 GERTRUDE JEKYLL PLAN
REDISCOVERED AND OBSESSIVELY
AND METICULOUSLY RE-CREATED
IN 1980S.

CLAREMONT LANDSCAPE
GARDEN AMPHITHEATRE OF
DOUBLE-STEPPED GRASSED
EARTHWORK IN SURREY (FAR
RIGHT) IS UNIQUE. 1740S
BAROQUE DESIGN CAN BE SEEN
NOW IN CONTEXT OF 1960S
LAND ART IN USA.

Introduction

The right style of landscape architecture for the twentieth century, and beyond, is no style at all, but a new conception of planning the human environment.
Christopher Tunnard

We are garden and landscape designers and, in the guise of our television personae, *The Curious Gardeners*, we have the most wonderful opportunity to explore the glorious gardens of Great Britain. As we travelled the length and breadth of the country looking at gardens for the new series, we were struck yet again by the sheer quantity of truly exciting gardens in Britain. We were also struck by their diversity. We only had time and space to show you a few of them, so we had to make difficult choices.

The gardens we looked at ranged from the great and grand to the small and individual, and covered every period from seventeenth-century formality through eighteenth-century Picturesque informality to the pervasive and persistent influence of the Arts and Crafts movement in the twentieth century, with its delight in the labour intensive herbaceous border.

Today, we are glad to say, gardens are changing again, as contemporary materials are used in new ways, and different styles of planting become more popular. Almost without exception, the gardens we saw reflected the prevailing fashions of the particular time at which they were made but, within this broad expression of fashion, individual gardeners always make their own personal, often idiosyncratic statements of style, choosing to emphasise particular aspects according to their individual tastes.

It would have been easy to consider the gardens simply in their historical context, but gradually it became apparent that the many different gardens were united by six elements that are common to all gardens, of

whatever period. These are the individual elements that any garden maker must take into account when planning a garden, even if they are not aware that they are doing so.

We have chosen to focus on these six elements (which are time, form, sculpture, water, materials and plants) in a complete range of gardens, from classic to modern. Although the way the elements are expressed may take different forms over the centuries, they are as relevant today as they have always been.

We have chosen more than forty gardens that embody the principles that make for good and often exciting garden design. Some of the gardens are already extremely well known, but we could not resist including them because they are such superb examples of the gardener's art. Others are private gardens, usually seen only by the lucky few. They can be broadly divided into the traditional and the contemporary, but this distinction can sometimes be misleading: traditional gardens

may contain surprisingly contemporary features, and contemporary gardens may be highly nostalgic. Through the six basic elements intrinsic to gardens of any period or style, we explore why these gardens are successful, stunning, amusing and quirky or simply breath-stoppingly beautiful. We have given the designer's name in the heading for each garden.

Time is perhaps the most important of all elements in a garden, yet it is rarely explored in books on garden design. It has many aspects and involves making important decisions before even beginning to make detailed plans. Gardens that rely on plants alone are highly ephemeral. Individual gardeners may try to impose their own vision on a particular piece of ground but, unless they plan for the long term, that vision will only be realised on a temporary basis: the effects of time cannot be easily controlled.

We found an interesting example of an attempt to re-

HADSPEN HOUSE, SOMERSET
TWENTY-FIRST-CENTURY
COLOUR SPECTRUM PLANTINGS
BRILLIANTLY SHOWN (LEFT) IN
WALLED GARDEN 'CANVAS' OF
NORI AND SANDRA POPE.
GARDENS OF GAIA SITE-
SPECIFIC SCULPTURES SUCH AS
KISSING ARCHWAY (BELOW),
WITTILY PLACED OVER A
NARROW STREAM IN TWENTY-
TWO ACRES OF KENT WOODS.
FLORA'S GARDEN
NORTHAMPTON GARDEN
TRANSFORMED FOR YOUNG
AUTISTIC GIRL (OPPOSITE)
IN A CIRCULAR CONCRETE
ENCLOSURE WITH FIBRE OPTICS
AND PROJECTED IMAGES TO
MAKE HER PRIVATE PLAY SPACE.

create time past in time present in the garden at Upton Grey in Hampshire, which is the most meticulous reconstruction of a Gertrude Jekyll plan from 1908. On the Scottish island of Bute, time past is still present in the 300-year-old aristocratic gardens at Mount Stuart, with its avenues of ancient trees. But we also discovered several fascinating examples of time moving on in this garden. An extensive potager made in 1991 (and the height of fashion at the time) was swept away less than ten years later, to be replaced by contemporary plantings with newly fashionable grasses. On the same estate a cutting-edge visitors' centre has stunning new gardens with the rows of planting based on the shape of a paper clip.

Changing the form of a garden is often the first major task that the garden maker undertakes. Form in the garden and landscape is a vast and complex subject and it comes in myriad shapes, both tangible (earth) and invisible (space). Essentially, it is about the relationship between the given space and its surroundings. The magnificent eighteenth-century grassed earthwork double amphitheatre built into a hillside at Claremont in Surrey has echoes in the National Botanic Garden of Wales, with its splendid twenty-first-century glasshouse. Here, earth was removed to make an arid canyon 5m (16ft) below ground level, thereby dramatically enhancing the earth form, but also increasing the sense of space, as well as altering magically the viewer's horizon line, under the vast glass roof – a unique example of moving earth to increase enclosed space.

Making the permanent features is usually the next stage of garden making. The traditional materials for hard landscaping were local stone and brick, but the range has broadened enormously in recent years as modern materials are brought into the garden, creating an entirely different look. The early twentieth-century formal garden at Hestercombe in Somerset is one of the supreme examples of the use of stone and its detailing. Classically inspired walls, terraces, steps, and copings are beautifully designed, using two types of local stone in many attractive forms. In complete contrast of style, but no less meticulous use of materials, is a new garden in Northampton for an autistic child. She has a secure circular concrete play area, which echoes a classical rotunda without the dome, with planting around the top, out of her reach. On the ground, coloured fibre optic lights play underneath glass blocks. Most engaging fun of all are the hidden wall projectors, which shoot out images across the area on to walls opposite.

Water was an essential feature in the very earliest gardens, and was a part of almost all the gardens we visited, in many conformations and configurations. We were mightily impressed by the formal eighteenth-century channelling of a river at Studley Royal in Yorkshire. The final shapes chosen by the aristocratic garden designer (yet another example of British divine amateurism?) are vast pools – one full moon flanked by two crescent moons – set in closely mown grass. There is a fabulous serenity here. A contrasting twentieth-century excitement with water is to be found in the garden at Shute House in Dorset, where the professional designer created a Mughal rill with Islamic pools on its course, making a silver ribbon through a lawn. The designer was inspired by a visit to Kashmir and the watercourses in the fabled Shalimar gardens on the edge of Lake Dal.

Sculpture, whether made of long-lasting materials such as stone or 'living' sculpture in the form of topiary, enhances any garden. In a traditional garden, sculptures were often used as focal points, to guide the eye within or beyond the garden, or as decoration for the out of doors. At Anglesey Abbey in Cambridgeshire, there seemed to be endless rows of imported Italian busts of the Roman emperors, marking out the vista along a grand avenue of

mainly Norway spruce and larch with some yew. In stark contrast with this traditional approach are the site-specific sculptures in a large patch of woodland in Kent. Making a sculpture inspired by the place where it is to be sited is a late-twentieth-century concept. Several sculptors have made haunting pieces inspired by spaces among the trees in the Gardens of Gaia.

Plants are vital to a garden, but planting is usually the final stage of making a garden, and cannot be done until all the hard landscaping is in place. Despite our reputation, we do truly know and understand the importance and value of plants, but only as one of the elements to be considered in any garden design. At Great Dixter in East Sussex, an early twentieth-century Arts and Crafts garden has many traditionally based plant elements and combinations, including yew hedge rooms and herbaceous borders, but part of the garden has been brought up to date with exotic plantings of canna lilies, banana

NORTH LONDON (LEFT)
TWENTY-FIRST-CENTURY
RISING GLASS BLOCK WALL
FRAMING GLASS CHADAR,
A CONTEMPORARY VARIATION
ON A SIXTEENTH-CENTURY
MUGHAL INDIAN STONE WATER
SLIDE OR CHUTE, HIGHLIT IN
THE EVENING BY FOUR SCENES
OF FIBRE OPTIC LIGHTING.
(OPPOSITE) GUY COOPER,
GORDON TAYLOR AND
ARCHITECT, SAL PATEL,
DESIGNED THIS TOWN GARDEN
FOR A YOUNG COUPLE
DARING TO COMMISSION A
CONTEMPORARY GARDEN IN
TANDEM WITH THEIR INTEREST
IN MODERN ART.

trees and other such subjects. For a brilliant contemporary use of plants in the herbaceous border genre, we love the walled gardens at Hadspen in Somerset, where superbly chosen and truly unusual plant combinations based on harmonious colour spectrums are planted most brilliantly for spring and summer.

> I want all my [gardens] to seem the homes of children and lovers. I want them to be comfortable and if possible slightly mysterious by day, with vistas and compositions appealing to the painter. I want them to be delirious by moonlight . . . I believe there is no beauty without ugliness and that it should not be otherwise. Both are capable of stinging us to live. Contrast is more true than undeviating smugness. The chief vice in gardens . . . is to be merely pretty.
>
> *Fletcher Steele*

These are the inspiring words of a major twentieth-century American landscape architect and designer, Fletcher Steele, who was much influenced by the great Art Deco exhibition of 1925 in Paris. It was one of the watersheds of Modernism, and the garden designs shown there are still revered by today's garden designers. We always try to bear them in mind when we are designing a garden.

Before the second television series was commissioned, we had been asked to make a garden in the centre of London for a young couple. Since he is English and she is Indian, they wanted an Anglo-Indian garden. The garden is a flat space 10m (35ft) wide and 15m (50ft) long, bounded by a few good mature trees, including a fig, an apple, a plum and a 6m (20ft) high bay tree. The owners have a small child. Her area now takes up approximately two thirds of the garden (we divided the garden plan by the Golden Section), and has a brand new lawn and a sandpit. The remaining third is tucked away behind a wonderful semicircular glass block wall. Here there is a raised area for dining and another area protected by the old fig tree for sitting and musing while children play.

Since the owners look down on the garden from rooms on the first floor of the house and above, we decided to create a central feature. We chose an adaptation of the chadar, which is a chute or waterslide used to take water from one level to another in Mughal gardens of the sixteenth century. The chute we designed is a contemporary version of the traditional stone chadar, made of clear toughened glass. It is 2m (6ft) wide and 4.2m (14ft) long, and descends from a height of 2.5m (8ft), with a recirculating pump in the main reservoir. During the day the water flows gently down the glass into a pool filled with rocks and small boulders from the same quarry as the gravel used on either side. It makes a soothing sound, and shines and ripples enchantingly over the glass; at night the underlighting makes the chadar waterfall truly magical.

On either side of the central lawn are two borders approximately 3m (10ft) long and 50cm (20in) wide, where a succession of flowering plants will give colour and scent to the garden during spring, summer and autumn (and will be tended by the owner's father). In one corner, a clipped yew spiral makes a focal point in front of a hedge of bamboos.

In one London garden are examples of all six of the elements that have driven both the television series and this book. The owners wanted an 'instant' garden, and the entire design took only seven weeks to install. The form of the flat, rectangular space has been altered by dividing it into separate areas and introducing a change of level, and the materials are both traditional and contemporary, being stone, cement, brick, gravel, glass and glass blocks. The chadar adds the essential element of water, and sculpture is present in the yew topiary. The established trees, the new bamboos and the annual plants both in the beds and in pots on the terrace make up the planting.

The gardens we have chosen here are exciting and inspiring. British gardens are the most diverse in the world, being blessed a with temperate climate and a long, splendid garden-making history that encompasses both the traditional and contemporary 🌱

Gordon Taylor   Guy Cooper

time

As the years pass by and no rude hand disturbs the traces in her presence,

Nature becomes more daring. Flower-spangled tapestries of woven tendrils fall from the terrace, . . .

the niches are curtained with creepers, the pool is choked with water plants,

blossoming weeds are in every crevice . . . Autumn has come at last . . .

Sir George Sitwell, *On the Making of Gardens* (1909)

SISSINGHURST GARDENS
(PREVIOUS PAGE) AN EPITOME
OF EARLY TWENTIETH-CENTURY
BRITISH GARDEN DESIGN –
FORMAL PLAN WITH INFORMAL
PLANTINGS – SET IN LUSH
FARMLANDS OF THE WEALD OF
KENT.

LEVENS HALL ARTIST JULIA
BARTON'S PHYTOFORMS (LEFT)
– PRESENT-DAY TOPIARY
SCULPTURES – ABSTRACT
CONSTRUCTIONS OF WIRE,
COMPOST AND DROUGHT-
RESISTANT PLANTS JUXTAPOSED
WITH BRITAIN'S MOST
IMPORTANT SEVENTEENTH-
CENTURY YEW AND BOX
TOPIARY.

Time may be the most important element in the garden. Every new garden starts as a fantasy in the mind of the owner, to be realised through a mixture of skills and vision, but Nature intervenes and makes certain no garden ever materialises exactly as initially imagined. All gardens change, season by season and year by year, and we hardly ever come across an owner who says, 'This is the perfect day for you to be here.' People usually say, 'Oh, you should have come two weeks ago', or 'My roses will look perfect next week.'

Houses may endure for many centuries, but gardens are transitory. If a garden is not tended on a regular basis, it will alter in six months and look decayed and unloved a year later. Eventually all that remains is its permanent structure, made up of hard surfaces such as paths and walls, together with any trees that have attained maturity. This is true of the Italian gardens that have inspired the rest of the gardening world over the last five centuries, and have survived despite neglect. These gardens are usually large, but they depend essentially on the organisation of views and vistas, using *allées* of trees and hedges with statues as eye-catchers, and glorious water features. Since these are a combination of hard landscaping and evergreen trees and plants, rather than flowers, they can be tidied up and restored comparatively easily.

British gardens, with their dependence on plants, both annuals and perennials, are much more transient. Time passes, and owners change. As an adolescent, Guy Cooper helped in the restoration and improvement of the large garden around the house in which he grew up. More than fifty years ago, he persuaded the gardener to move a line of runner beans which could be seen from the drawing room. A few years later, the house was sold and eventually torn down, but when he visited the garden again recently, someone else had planted runner beans in exactly the same position from which he had ordered them to be removed . . .

Even if there are plans of what was once intended, we usually do not know how accurately these were carried out. At Upton Grey in Hampshire, Gertrude Jekyll's original plans for two perennial borders and much else, designed in 1908, have been scrupulously reinstated almost eighty years later. What we see now is what Miss Jekyll hoped would be seen.

Gardens usually change with their owners, because different people have different fantasies, different wishes and ideals. Owners of a garden have the right, the *droite de proprietaire*, to conceive, install and maintain a garden as they wish it to be. The styles of a number of historical eras are wonderfully expressed in the gardens at Sissinghurst Castle in Kent, although they are really out of historical phase. Its sixteenth-century tower and outbuildings have been given an Italianate feel, but the gardens in which they are set were designed in the early twentieth century in the Arts and Crafts style. They were designed at a particular moment in time, and are a reflection of that time.

When designers such as Capability Brown planned grand landscapes in previous centuries, he had a different perspective. He and his clients knew that they would not live to see, say, their treescapes in maturity. It was of no importance, because they were certain the same families would continue to live, generation by generation, looking at the same views (even if their belief was mistaken). The passage of time in gardens and landscapes can be seen over any number of timescales, and sometimes change comes slowly. Centuries of time are the agreed markers at both Mount Stuart, on the Isle of Bute in Scotland, with its magnificent avenues of mature trees planted some three hundred years ago, and at Levens Hall in Cumbria, where the splendid yew topiary is just a few decades older. But even these ancient gardens evolve with time, and contemporary styles are beginning to intervene.

When we design gardens for clients today, we know that some of them want the mature garden 'yesterday'. Few of them have that essential ingredient of gardening which is PATIENCE, and most of them are unlikely to be living in the same house in ten years' time. The amount of time that people can spend looking after their gardens has also changed radically in the last hundred years, and many now wish to have gardens that are as simple as possible to maintain. Contemporary techniques of growing and establishing plants, trees and shrubs have made it possible to create an instantly mature landscape, albeit at some cost. But it is much more satisfactory to allow the view from a house to grow, change and mature over at least five years.

In terms of horticultural planting, such timescales are minuscule, but we have to be realistic about people's wishes and whims and try to encourage the new gardener to be realistic, in turn, about how soon their fantasies will become reality. Another approach is to turn this notion on its head, as Adrian Fisher has done with his maize mazes, which are designed to last for a single season. His fantasies are realised within a year or less, and the passing of time offers him endless excitement.

Wherever you garden, we think there is something very romantic about the change and decay of a garden. A lady in North Yorkshire, whose husband had been a celebrated plantsman, would take visitors round her garden, where she had lived for forty years, and talk about it as though it was still looking as it did in its heyday. She ignored the trees that had grown too tall, the shrubs that spilled over on to the pathway, the perennials overgrown with weeds and the water feature that no longer worked. In her eyes, it was still as perfect as her husband had wanted it to be, and that enthusiasm was transmitted to us by her nostalgia for a moment in time that only she remembers

GROUP OF PLANTS (RIGHT)
PLACED EXACTLY BY ROS
WALLINGER ACCORDING TO
GERTRUDE JEKYLL'S 1908 PLAN;
A TOTAL RE-CREATION.

ONE OF MISS JEKYLL'S
FAVOURITE VERTICAL PLANTS,
THE YUCCA, IN THE
FOREGROUND OF A BORDER
DESIGN (OPPOSITE) RUNNING
OUT FROM THE UPTON GREY
ARTS AND CRAFTS HOUSE, SET
IN A JEYKLL GARDEN, THE
PERFECT TRADITIONAL BRITISH
COUNTRYSIDE PICTURE.

The Manor House

UPTON GREY, HAMPSHIRE

Rosamund Wallinger and Gertrude Jekyll

In 1984 the Wallingers were looking for a fairly large country house within easy commuting distance of London. They found a dilapidated property at Upton Grey, a small village near Basingstoke in Hampshire. Originally a sixteenth-century manor, the house was enlarged and redesigned at the end of the nineteenth century for a wealthy textile merchant, Charles Holme, founder of the arts journal *The Studio*, and is now a very fine example of an Arts and Crafts house by the important architect in that style, Ernest Newton. Rosamund Wallinger was not a gardener at all when she and her husband bought the property but, in the course of restoring the house, they found a plan at the Royal Institute of British Architects on which was written 'garden possibly by Gertrude Jekyll'.

Both Newton and Holme were acquainted with Gertrude Jekyll, who had given up being a painter and embroiderer when her eyesight became too weak for close work and had taken up designing gardens instead. By the time she met Edwin Lutyens in 1889, she was already well known for her designs for herbaceous borders. He was a young but promising architect aged only twenty, while she was in her forties, but they collaborated wonderfully on house and garden projects until her death in 1932. She merited a splendid obituary in *The Times*:

Gertrude Jekyll, to whom we now bid a grateful 'Hail and Farewell', sought ever for practical knowledge allied to beauty, and in that quest, whereby she may truly be said to have transfigured the gardens of England, she never grew old at heart or wearied in mind, was never discouraged by difficulty or defeated by failure, neither did she cease to share widely the fruits of her long and loving apprenticeship to Nature.

Gertrude Jekyll was one of many garden designers for the rich and famous in Edwardian times, but her name has come down to us when those of her contemporaries are long forgotten because she also wrote a series of splendid books. These have been in print almost continuously for most of the last hundred years and are still read today, and so her name has been immortalised.

The mention of Gertrude Jekyll's name on the plan alerted Rosamund Wallinger, who asked the Hampshire Gardens Trust whether they had any information about the garden. Fortunately, they knew that more than 2,000 of Gertrude Jekyll's drawings of garden designs and planting plans for about 250 gardens had been sold to an American landscape architect, Mrs Beatrix Farrand, as part of a fundraising effort for the British Red Cross at the beginning of the Second World War. On her death in 1959, Mrs Farrand bequeathed them to the Reef Point Collection held at the University of California, Berkeley,

in the United States. The *cognoscenti* know that her drawings are there and, as they have recently been put on microfilm, they are now available for anybody who wishes to study them. A few years ago, another 150 drawings by Gertrude Jekyll were found in an attic in Surrey by one of her descendants, thus increasing the amount of archival material available for anybody wishing to reinstate one of her gardens.

Having enlisted the help of Penelope Hobhouse, Rosamund Wallinger wrote to Berkeley; eighteen plans arrived two months later. By that time Mrs Wallinger had started to uncover the completely overgrown garden at the back of the house and had found three major drystone retaining walls that divided the area into a series of terraces, descending to a tennis lawn. These were in such poor condition that they needed to be entirely rebuilt. The walls were originally of Purbeck and Bargate stone but fifty years on Bargate stone is

RAMPANT LAVENDER, RED
HOT POKERS AND HOLLYHOCKS
(LEFT) IN ONE OF THE MISS
JEKYLL BORDERS AT UPTON
GREY.

IMAGE OF THE UR-PLAN OF
THE ROSE LAWN AT UPTON
GREY BY GERTRUDE JEKYLL
(BELOW LEFT)

PERFECT JEKYLLIAN GARDEN
PICTURE AT UPTON GREY
(OPPOSITE): A DREAMY BRITISH
LANDSCAPE BEYOND YEW
HEDGES AND LONG FLOWER
BORDERS ENCLOSES A SUNKEN
LAWN WITH PAEONY, ROSE AND
LILY BEDS.

almost unobtainable. However, she and a young builder nicknamed Derek 'the Walls' were able to dismantle what remained of the walls and build them again using the same stone, so that the structural outlines of Gertrude Jekyll's design were re-created.

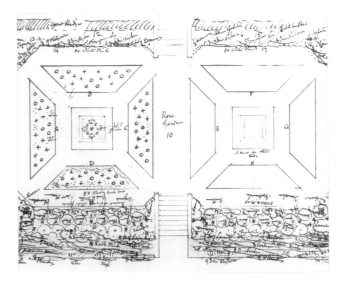

As Rosamund Wallinger studied the drawings, she realised that they were only working plans and the handwriting was almost indecipherable. However, they dated from 1908, when Miss Jekyll was at the height of her powers. By then she and Lutyens had designed the gardens at Hestercombe (generally considered to be their greatest achievement) and she had just published her great book on the herbaceous border, *Colour in the Flower Garden* (1908). Mrs Wallinger was determined to proceed, and by 1986 she had started to set out the two long borders at the back of the house according to the original planting plans. She also replanted the formal rose garden on the terrace between the borders, with its central raised beds of lilies and paeonies.

Between the front of the house and the road, Gertrude Jekyll had planted a more informal wilderness area, reached along winding paths that lead from the house down to a pond sheltered by trees. In 1999 a

living willow arbour was reinstated in the wilderness, making a bower seat for two. Four drifts of climbing roses interrupt the view of the churchyard which is immediately next to the informal part of the garden, and in one area they frame the church door.

From photographs taken when Charles Holme was living there, it is extremely likely that he was less fastidious in following Gertrude Jekyll's plans than Rosamund Wallinger has been. Holme had nine gardeners where Mrs Wallinger has only one, but she admits that her obsession with the garden is such that she spends every available moment of her life tending it, working alongside her gardener. It is extremely rare that the owner of a historical house and garden wishes to recreate a landscape that was designed eight decades previously, and does so in such a complete and lovingly detailed way. Usually a new owner prefers to impress their own personality upon the garden and the surrounding landscape, but here the owner has decided to re-create and maintain another person's fantasy.

Rosamund Wallinger's work is truly wondrous in its meticulous detail and splendid energy. Nothing on the original plan has been altered or changed, and everything has been planted as Rosamund Wallinger thinks Gertrude Jekyll would have wished it to be, using only those plants that existed in 1908 (and now Mrs Wallinger knows where such plants are to be found). So second time around and nearly eighty years later, the Jekyll borders have been planted and maintained as she would have wished, down to the last lily (in full bloom with wonderful scent on the day we visited) and the final lamb's ear. About four thousand people a year visit this amazing reconstruction which puts up a brave fight against that most ancient enemy of the garden, time

GLASGOW GARDEN FESTIVAL

CONTEMPORARY ART

INSTALLATION OF INSCRIBED
SAND ON LAWN IN FRONT OF
GREAT MOUNT STUART HOUSE
(RIGHT). THE SHAPES ARE BASED
ON A BRONZE AGE CELTIC
NECKLACE FOUND ON THE ISLE
OF BUTE.

ROMAN-STYLE COLUMN

FOCAL POINT (OPPOSITE) IS
DEDICATED BY THE EIGHTEENTH-
CENTURY EARL OF BUTE TO
AUGUSTA, DOWAGER PRINCESS
OF WALES, MOTHER OF
GEORGE III; SHE AND THE
EARL WERE CO-FOUNDERS
OF KEW GARDENS.

GLASGOW GARDEN FESTIVAL

PAVILION (OVERLEAF) NOW
HOUSES SUB-TROPICAL PLANTS.
MUCH CHANGE HERE –
BOXWOOD HEDGES INSTALLED
IN THE EARLY 1990S FOR A
POTAGER ARE NO LONGER
WANTED AND NOW ENCLOSE
FASHIONABLE GRASSES AND
PERENNIALS.

Mount Stuart

ISLE OF BUTE, SCOTLAND

James Alexander-Sinclair

' Mount Stuart has always been a place for innovation. If you look at the architecture, the gardens, there is passion and conviction. We didn't want it all to become a time capsule, to become preserved in aspic for ever.'
James Alexander-Sinclair on Mount Stuart

Nobody knows exactly how long the Butes have lived on the Isle of Bute, but they have certainly been there for seven or eight hundred years. Originally they lived in the town of Rothesay, but at the beginning of the eighteenth century they moved about 16km (10 miles) down the coast and built a large mansion called Mount Stuart. Then they set about the policies, as the parkland around a stately home is known in Scotland. The word 'policies' is based on the Latin word *politus*, which means 'embellishment' and so is a very correct word to describe the grounds around this grand house.

There is a large open space leading down to the sea from the garden side of the house, and woods were planted on either side of this open space by the 2nd Earl when the house was built. (When we visited, a large image of a Celtic necklace found at the property had been drawn in sand on the lawn; this temporary installation may yet become permanent.) Later in the eighteenth century, two avenues were made at the end of the lawn, parallel to the house, one called the Lime Avenue and the other the Forty-Five Avenue. A little way from the beginning of the Forty-Five Avenue is a column which was originally at Luton Hoo in Bedfordshire (one of the 3rd Earl's homes in England). The statue on top represents a Roman notable, but the column is dedicated to the mother of George III, Augusta, Dowager Princess of Wales, to whom the earl was devoted. The two of them were responsible for the establishment of the Royal Botanic Gardens at Kew,

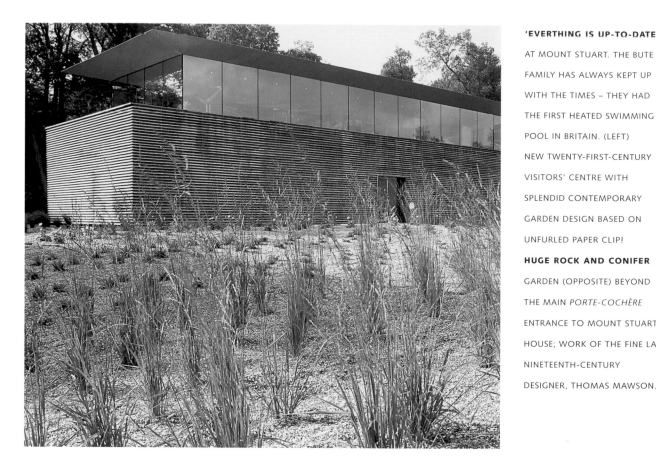

'EVERTHING IS UP-TO-DATE'
AT MOUNT STUART. THE BUTE
FAMILY HAS ALWAYS KEPT UP
WITH THE TIMES – THEY HAD
THE FIRST HEATED SWIMMING
POOL IN BRITAIN. (LEFT)
NEW TWENTY-FIRST-CENTURY
VISITORS' CENTRE WITH
SPLENDID CONTEMPORARY
GARDEN DESIGN BASED ON
UNFURLED PAPER CLIP!
HUGE ROCK AND CONIFER
GARDEN (OPPOSITE) BEYOND
THE MAIN *PORTE-COCHÈRE*
ENTRANCE TO MOUNT STUART
HOUSE; WORK OF THE FINE LATE
NINETEENTH-CENTURY
DESIGNER, THOMAS MAWSON.

which have since become one of the most important horticultural centres in the world.

In 1823, Maria North, wife of the 5th Earl, created the Wee Garden, which is a microclimate within the wooded landscape of the estate. An extensive collection of semi-hardy shrubs and trees from South Africa and South America was planted here. A burn or stream, known as the Racers Burn, runs through these gardens, and in the centre is a sundial dating from the seventeenth century.

When the 3rd Marquis was rebuilding the house after a fire in 1896, he asked Thomas Mawson to create a rock garden on a hill outside the grand entrance to the house. A stream flowing down the slope was turned into a series of water features and pools, and enormous rocks were imported and positioned so as to look as though they had always been there. The garden fell out of fashion during the 1920s and 30s and became neglected, but Eileen, wife of the 5th Marquis, restored the gardens after the Second World War. In the 1980s, the 6th Marchioness added a magnificent collection of 1,500 different plants from the Near and Far East.

When the 6th Marquis inherited the house in the 1980s, he and his wife realised that the whole garden – the policies as well as the pleasure gardens – had fallen into decay and needed a lot of restoration and revision. The old vegetable garden was no longer needed to feed the family and staff, so the lord and lady had the idea of turning it into a more decorative area. In 1988 they installed a metal-framed pavilion, originally made for the Glasgow Garden Festival. The pavilion is now a tropical microclimate in which a range of plants that enjoy such humid conditions are grown. Then they contacted the late Rosemary Verey and asked her to install a large version of one of her 'retro' historical potagers around this pavilion. She designed it so that there were eight

areas, two for herbs and the rest for either vegetables or flowers for the house.

In 2000, James Alexander-Sinclair, an old friend of the incumbent marquis, was asked to review the state of the policies and the rest of the landscape at Mount

FOR JAMES ALEXANDER-SINCLAIR, CONSTANT EVOLUTION IS THE ESSENCE OF KEEPING A GARDEN ALIVE AND CONTEMPORARY.

Stuart. He decided that all the vegetables and flowers could be banished from Verey's parterres, to be replaced with a series of beds filled with perennials and grasses that would sway pleasantly in the breeze during several months of the year and would need much less maintenance. A large ornamental vegetable garden had come and gone in barely ten years.

Immediately across the road from this garden, a new

and very contemporary visitors' centre, designed by Munkenbeck and Marshall, was built in twelve months and opened in May 2001. Below it James Alexander-Sinclair has planted an area inspired by an unfurled paper clip, which has been formally planted with vertical flower spikes and grasses, chosen to contrast with the horizontal building. All these plants grow through gravel, which reduces weeds and maintenance.

One of the designer's main priorities is the continuing renewal of this amazing landscape: many of the trees in the policies are now almost three hundred years old and will soon need to be replaced. He recognises that landscapes are always changing and that in only a few decades what he has done will be changed again. For James Alexander-Sinclair, constant evolution is the essence of keeping a garden alive and contemporary. We think this is one of the wisest descriptions of landscape design we have heard for a very long time 🌱

OCTAGONAL **PAVILION** FOR
WRITING AND MUSING (RIGHT)
BUILT BY NIGEL NICOLSON IN
HONOUR OF HIS FATHER, SIR
HAROLD, WHO WAS DESIGNER
OF THE FORMAL PLAN FOR THE
GARDENS AT SISSINGHURST.
BOAT HOUSE OF MOST STURDY
BRITISH OAK (OPPOSITE) AT THE
TOP OF SISSINGHURST MOAT;
IT WAS BUILT BY THE NICOLSON
FAMILY TO MARK THE
MILLENNIUM.

Sissinghurst Castle

CRANBROOK, KENT

Harold Nicolson and Vita Sackville-West

'People who like to boast of their long and deep acquaintance with the place are apt to say that Sissinghurst is no longer what it was "in Vita's day", implying that it has lost something of its serenity and betrayed her genius. Let the reply be this: that no garden is, or should ever be, what it was, since it is a living, growing, changing thing, and it would be foolish, unimaginative and actually treacherous to Vita's own conception of a garden to replace every plant that dies and every tree that topples over by the same plant or the same tree.'

Nigel Nicolson on Sissinghurst Castle

On 4th April 1930, Vita Sackville-West and her son, Nigel Nicolson, drove through Kent from Long Barn, where they were then living, to Sissinghurst Castle. Vita and her husband, Harold Nicolson, had decided that they needed a new home as there was likely to be a housing development around Long Barn. That day, Nigel and his mother looked at an Elizabethan tower with three floors above a very grand archway. Little else remained of the grand Elizabethan house, and the other buildings were crumbling and surrounded by the detritus of an abandoned farm: old farm machinery, broken carts and mounds of rubbish. Vita had only been there for a little while when she turned to Nigel and said, 'Darling, we will be very happy here,' and they drove away. A month later, the Nicolsons had bought the castle and the surrounding land, and two years later they moved in.

The family had somewhat strange living arrangements. Vita and Harold had their bedrooms in what was known as the South Cottage, overlooking a small garden which was always planted with brilliant flowers in yellow, orange and red. Their two sons and the rest of the household lived in the Priest's House and in what had been the old stable block. At the same time as the

GREAT DOORWAY AT THE BASE
OF SISSINGHURST CASTLE
CENTRAL TOWER HOUSED THE
STUDY OF VITA SACKVILLE-
WEST, THE OTHER CREATOR OF
THE GARDENS WITH HER
AMAZING PLANTINGS.
SOUTH COTTAGE GARDEN
(OPPOSITE BELOW) WHERE WE
WERE AMAZED, TWENTY-FIVE
YEARS AGO, AT SEEING THE
VERMILION CLIMBING
NASTURTIUM BLAZING UP THESE
WONDERFUL DARK GREEN YEWS.

living accommodation was being rebuilt, Harold designed the garden.

Harold Nicolson was a classicist, and much influenced by the gardens of the Italian Renaissance. His idea was that there should be ten separate gardens – some square, some oblong, one circular – divided by walls and buildings (mainly extant), or by hedges. All the enclosed areas were to have views through them so that each garden could be seen either along a vista or from different perspectives. For example, there is a view from the great archway through the orchard towards a statue of Dionysus, placed on the far side of a moat. In another part of the garden is an *allée* which also has the statue as its focal point, but from a quite different point of view. This was Harold Nicolson's skill.

Nigel Nicolson helped his father lay out the garden, which includes a transverse yew *allée* that is approximately 60m (200ft) long, with a seat at one end and a statue at the other as an eye-catcher. Of course, it was a bare field when Nigel, directed by his father, stood holding the end of a piece of string where the *allée* was to finish. Alas, they got it slightly wrong and the *allée* is almost 60cm (2ft) off centre. Nigel Nicolson remembers his mistake fondly, and doubts whether many visitors notice it.

Vita's genius was filling Harold's geometric spaces with an abundance of flowers, shrubs and trees. She loved plants and used them enthusiastically. Each garden was discovered by a grass path, but the flowers were encouraged to leap over the box hedges that edged the beds and on to the paths, growing where they might.

Such was the fame of Sissinghurst that people longed to see it and so the garden was opened to the public in 1946. The visitors were known by the family as the Sixpennies, since they each had to put sixpence into the collection box. Vita began writing a regular article about the garden in a Sunday newspaper, and more and more people came to look at it. Even she realised that some of the grass paths would have to be replaced by paths with hard surfaces to accommodate the visitors. Vita died in 1962 but she had been helped in her last years by two gardeners, Pam Schwerdt and Sibylle Kreutzberger, who continued looking after the garden for nearly thirty more years.

All gardens change. When Nigel Nicolson inherited Sissinghurst, he decided to transfer the property to the National Trust, and this was done in 1967. Soon, the garden was being visited by more people than any other owned by the National Trust. The two gardeners inevitably had to make changes. Some were purely practical, and others became necessary as plants died and were replaced, but the two ladies were as scrupulous as possible in choosing plants that they thought Vita would have liked. They finally retired in 1991, after many years of sensitive stewardship in this garden dream, and the garden is now looked after by Sarah Cook, who also chooses plants which reflect Vita's personality and aesthetics, rather than plants that may be fashionable at the beginning of the twenty-first century. Sarah has an interesting view of time in the garden:

> One of the great things about gardening as an art form is the number of different time dimensions that you are working within. You are working from minute to minute, from day to day, from week to week, from season to season. As the seasons change, you are working from year to year, over something like a three-year period. And also a hundred-year period. If a tree grows, it takes perhaps fifty years to grow and then it dies and suddenly you've got an area that needs complete change. So, you have many fascinating different timescales to work within.

Perhaps the best-known area of the gardens at Sissinghurst is the White Garden, which started as a rose garden and was then replanted in white by Vita in about 1950. The immense white *Rosa mulliganii* in the centre now grows over a gothic arbour and was still in flower when we were there in mid-July, but other planting has been changed as Vita Sackville-West becomes a more distant memory. The changes reflect the need for the garden to have white flowers for most of the year, in order to please its many visitors. Since Vita's death in 1962, a number of plants that are now identified with Sissinghurst have been introduced. These include *Verbena* 'Sissinghurst' in the 1970s, *Thalictrum acquilegifolium* 'White Cloud' after 1977 and *Phlox* 'Violet Vere' in 1986.

Nigel Nicolson still lives at Sissinghurst, and says that he knows the gardens are in good hands. He has added an octagonal pavilion where the moat turns at a right angle, as a memorial to his father. This is a place where he may now write in solitude, because like his father and all his children, Nigel Nicolson has always written and continues to do so. To celebrate the millennium, he built a boathouse where the moat begins. This has yet to be used, but only because an engineering defect has made it impossible to row a boat from the boathouse along the moat. But this will soon be changed, and so a moat that has been there for four hundred years will become a place where Nigel or his descendants may take a gentle ride in the evening  and gaze up at the tower of Sissinghurst Castle. Sissinghurst may be considered the epitome of the English garden, with its strong architectural plan and its rich variety of plants, but the garden continues to evolve ❧

TWENTY-FIRST-CENTURY

TOPIARY SCULPTURE (RIGHT)

DESIGNED BY ARTIST JULIA

BARTON, INSPIRED BY LADIES IN

GRAND DRESSES DRAWN ON A

LATE EIGHTEENTH-CENTURY

PLAN IN THE HALL AT LEVENS.

FORMALISED VEGETABLE

BORDER PLANTINGS (OPPOSITE

BELOW) NESTLING NEAR SOME

OF THE VENERABLE YEW HEDGES

FORMING THE LARGE GARDEN

COMPARTMENTS AT LEVENS.

VIEW OF MAIN TOPIARY

GARDEN AT LEVENS HALL

(OVERLEAF) DATING FROM LAST

DECADE OF THE SEVENTEENTH

CENTURY; NOTE THE

HEXAGONAL TREE SEAT UNDER

GIANT TOPIARY ON RIGHT.

Levens Hall

KENDAL, CUMBRIA

Julia Barton

'I want to play with manmade materials and plant forms. I think there's a long way to go and I've got lots of ideas about it. I think topiary in the traditional sense can take on new forms, more abstract forms than it ever has in the past.'

Julia Barton on Levens Hall

There has been a house on the site of Levens Hall since the thirteenth century but most of the present house dates from the late sixteenth century, and was obviously built by a man of means. Some of the panelling of that time is still in place and there is much fine late-sixteenth- and seventeenth-century furniture. In 1694, the owners asked Guillaume Beaumont, who had been gardener to James II, to help them create a contemporary garden around their house. He decided the main area of the garden should be divided into four, with a large beech circle in the middle, and each of those squares was further divided by paths into four quarters. Today, one of the original squares is a bowling green, another is an orchard, the third contains a circular fountain which was reinstated in 1994, and the fourth contains an oblong vegetable potager, a herb garden and a nuttery.

Topiary was the height of fashion at the time, following the arrival of William of Orange from the Netherlands in 1688 with his wife, Mary, to become King and Queen of Great Britain. Suddenly everything Dutch was fashionable. Gardens were planted with beautiful rows of long, clipped hedges, and formal examples of topiary, either in yew or box, were set in the spaces between them, to bewitch the eye. Between 1694 and 1712, Beaumont made a topiary garden to the side of the house, and twenty-five of the yews that he planted there over three hundred years ago still remain. They are the historic basis of the magnificent topiary sculptures at Levens Hall.

The fashion for topiary soon passed, and by the middle of the eighteenth century the Picturesque style, which was extremely naturalistic, had swept away almost all the formal gardens around the great houses of England. However, the gardens at Levens Hall were not altered, either because the owners were happy with what they inherited or because they had insufficient money to change them. The topiary was well maintained, and today it is still as shown on the first plan of the gardens, which dates from the early nineteenth century.

There is no means of knowing what images Beaumont originally intended the topiary to replicate. Many of the ancient topiaries have grown as they will and now resemble multi-tiered umbrellas. There are two very large pieces which are known as the King and Queen since they somewhat resemble pieces from a chessboard. The family call another of them Queen Elizabeth the First and her Maids of Honour. One resembles the Howard Lion from the family's crest, and yet another is called the Judge's Wig. For the rest, they are large, beautifully maintained, but more abstract shapes, now quite close together.

In the past few years the current head gardener, Chris Crowder, has planted fifteen new topiary, so there are now about 125 topiaries of various shapes and ages at Levens Hall. This is quite deliberate, because people visit the garden to admire the topiary and why should there not be new shapes as well as old for them to see and enjoy as they change from decade to decade?

In 2001, eight contemporary topiary (called Phytoforms by their creator) were placed in the garden. They were designed by Julia Barton, who was the artist-in-residence at Levens Hall at the time. She had known the garden for many years and had always been intrigued by the topiary. The new topiaries were made out of the hidden metal frames that are sometimes necessary to maintain the shape of these ancient shrub sculptures. (Many of the hedges also date back to the end of the seventeenth century and they, too, have to be wired and supported, so that they look tailored and serene on the outside, whatever their inner structure may contain.)

Julia is fascinated by what is seen and what is hidden, and her sculptures focus both on the form of the internal structure and the way it can be further embellished and completed with plants. Many of the plants she uses are succulents, which need little watering or maintenance once they are established on the compost within the frames. Some of her planting is almost carpet-bedding in style, but the sculptures look perfectly at home in the great circle in the middle of the grand plan.

Two more of her large Phytoform topiary stand at the front of the house, outside the main entrance. A fleeting glance gives the impression that they are two historical ladies with great skirts and cinched waists, and Julia's inspiration for these forms was two such ladies depicted in one of the earliest engravings of the gardens, which can be seen in the house. These twenty-first-century topiary ladies seem to be welcoming visitors into a garden that has been here for more than three hundred years, as part of a happy marriage between past and present

DOWN VIEW OF 'GREEN
ROOM' ATRIUM GARDEN
(RIGHT) ON THE TOP FLOOR
OF A LONDON HOTEL FOR
RELAXATION AND COCKTAILS –
YES, THERE IS A YANKEE-STYLE
WET BAR.

'GREEN ROOM' OFF THE MAIN
HOTEL CORRIDOR (OPPOSITE)
DESIGNED WITH MODULAR
FABRICATED METAL UNITS FOR
SEATING AND PLANTING
CONTAINERS, INCLUDES METAL
FRAMES FOR CLIMBERS WITH
LIGHTING.

The Leonard Hotel

MAYFAIR, LONDON

Paul Cooper

'Digging holes in the ground and laying turf, the traditional long-term way of making a garden, is not really
me at all. This is me in my element: we design it, prefab-
ricate it in steel, plant it and install it all in a few days.
Quick. Instantaneous, portability, transient or, even,
throwaway were words you'd never traditionally associ-
ate with the garden. For me, they are an essential part of
what I do, because they reflect contemporary lifestyle.'
Paul Cooper on The Leonard Hotel

Paul Cooper established his name with a series
of provocative gardens at the Chelsea Flower
Show. One design, called the Cool and Sexy
Garden, included an evocation of Marilyn Monroe, and
the garden that was installed was significantly different
from the one that had been approved by the Royal
Horticultural Society committee. All Paul Cooper's
designs are both contemporary and eccentric, and they
are based on his earlier experiences, first as a theatre
designer and then as a sculptor. He freely admits that he
is not a straightforward plant and soil man, but he is
very intrigued by the way contemporary materials and
shapes can give his clients an instant garden. Today
there is even more pressure on time than there was ten
years ago. Most people are at their offices earlier and
work later and the amount of quality time (to use the
ghastly, unmodified, politically correct phrase from the
United States) that people have is notably reduced.
People tend to want everything yesterday.

When a new top floor was being added to a hotel in
central London, the wife of the owner suggested that
there should be a small outdoor area with plants, where
the guests could meet for drinks and conversation. Paul
Cooper was called in, and the Green Room at the
Leonard Hotel was soon conceived, planned and
approved. The area is only 3m (10ft) wide and 5m (16ft)

ALL PAUL COOPER'S DESIGNS ARE BOTH
CONTEMPORARY AND ECCENTRIC,
AND THEY ARE BASED ON HIS EARLIER
EXPERIENCES, FIRST AS A THEATRE
DESIGNER AND THEN AS A SCULPTOR.

long, and is entered through one of the many doors in a long corridor, thus at first sight appearing to be another bedroom. It took about three weeks for the precision-made materials to be manufactured so that they would fit exactly into the confined space, and they were installed in three days.

Calling the garden the Green Room reminds people of the traditional area where actors and actresses meet and relax backstage. A great deal about this area is theatrical. The tall, metal-framed columns around which clematis climb contain lighting features that give a cool blue glow as evening becomes night but do not burn the plants. The plant holders are made of stainless steel, the floor and seats are honed Hopton limestone, their backs and some of the lighting fixtures are glass, and wire trellis on the wall supports climbing plants as well as pictures of brightly coloured plants. Paul is experimenting with evergreens such as bamboos and ivies, and he is also trying lavender, because he loves the scent.

Some of the plants may have to be changed if they do not survive the uncertain conditions, but that is what instantaneous gardening is all about. The days when people would plant their gardens for their children, or take the time to grow plants from seeds and cuttings, are going. People are willing and able to spend more money so that the outdoor room they want can be instantaneous. Anyone visiting the Green Room will be seduced into believing that the garden has been there for a long time

MAIZE MAZE 2001, CREATED
BY ADRIAN FISHER IN SUSSEX
WAS A COWBOY ON A REARING
HORSE AND (RIGHT) THE BOOT
HILL SIGN CONTINUES THE WILD
WEST THEME.

RAISED BRIDGES (OPPOSITE),
A FEATURE OF MAIZE MAZES
TO HELP FIND THE 'LOST' MAZE
VOYAGERS AND TO VIEW THE
PATTERN FROM A LOW BIRD'S-
EYE-VIEW.

Maize Maze

CRAWLEY, WEST SUSSEX

Adrian Fisher

drian Fisher has been making mazes all over the world for the last twenty years. The smallest may be a 4.5m (15ft) square maze on the cruise ship *Tampa*, called Arrow 25, and the largest at Millets Farm, Oxfordshire, which covers more than eight acres and has over 6km (3¾ miles) of paths. Some of the mazes last only a year (the ones made of maize are an example) and some, made as an installation for a party or an art exhibition, have even shorter lives. But, as Adrian Fisher remarked to us, what a way to start a party!

Mazes are derived from labyrinths, the earliest of which are found in designs that are almost 7,000 years old. Labyrinths were always variations on seven circles and had only one starting point. However twisted the path may be, it will lead inevitably from the exterior to the centre of the labyrinth. Mazes are similar but different. They were first made in Renaissance Italy and in the Netherlands, where they were created from tall hedges.

The difference is that mazes have options and they contain dead ends, so that the explorer may need to make several attempts before finding the correct path and may never reach the centre of the maze. William and Mary built a huge maze at Het Loo Palace in the Netherlands in 1682 and created a new maze at Hampton Court Palace in 1702. They continued to be made in English gardens for the next few decades, but many disappeared with the introduction of the Picturesque landscape in the middle of the eighteenth century. Now people are creating them again.

Adrian Fisher never knows what he may be asked to design. One client, who is obsessed with cricket, has a maze which shows giant stumps and a ball bouncing out of the landscape (the ball alone is 36m (120ft) in diameter). The visitor is let in through a wicket gate and, on finally reaching the centre, finds the family coat of arms, which consist of two dragons, gushing water.

There is also a cricket pavilion, so the owner can sit and have a gin and tonic on reaching his destination. As Adrian Fisher says, 'The pleasure when you welcome your guests to any garden is to say, "Come and play in my garden." And what is more playful than a maze? The joy of owning your own maze is looking at the faces of your guests as they come and discover it.'

At Tulley's Farm, Adrian Fisher makes a new maze on the 3 hectare (7 acre) site each year. In 2001, he created a maize maze of a cowboy on a rearing horse. It was constructed around a number of bridges, which formed a sort of Spaghetti Junction. There were four paths that went over the bridges and four further paths that crossed under them, so his maze voyagers had a choice of going up or going through. There were towers and lookouts for people who really were too amazed by the maze. They could climb up to see where they were and how they could get out.

The fastest person running around one of Adrian Fisher's maize mazes might reach the centre in six minutes, but it usually takes up to two hours. They are designed as a wonderful day out for families of different generations. Grandparents always think they know the way but they don't, as their grandchildren soon find out. Visitors are given bamboo sticks with flags on them so that a family member who gets lost can wave a flag and hope to be found, or the bewildered family can see other families waving at them from other parts of the site. In England, maize grows up to 2.75m (9ft) tall, but in North America it can grow as high as 3.5m (11ft), and the barriers are tough enough to withstand quite a lot of frolicking children and confused adults. The mazes attract at least 40,000 people each year and there are dedicated mazers and maze-makers who cannot wait to embark on the new voyage the following year.

Optical mazes, designed to be looked at rather than

walked through, are a good way of making a maze in a small area. Looking down on the maze from above, the eye follows and finds the path from the beginning to the centre. Lady Salisbury has recently created an optical maze in the gardens outside Hatfield House using box, which can also be used for larger mazes. More space is needed for a maze made of hedges. Here the controlling factor is the size of the hedge, which is usually 60cm (2ft) wide, and of the path, which is up to 90cm (3ft) wide. Realistically, Adrian Fisher thinks that you need a space of 30m (100ft) square to make a hedge maze, but games can be played in smaller areas. Paths can be used in both directions, or they may be colour coded so that the maze is a sequence of coloured paths, and physical barriers don't exist.

Some mazes are made of turf with gravel between grass paths but Adrian Fisher has reversed this so the paths are gravel and the turf is raised above. However many people visit the maze, the grass remains undisturbed and is easier to cut. He experiments endlessly with living plant materials and unchanging stable materials (stone, tile and metal). Other materials include water, with little jets and fountains that rise, or mirrors that give the sensation of a barrier or an opening. He has even designed a mathematical maze which has twenty-four different starting points, each providing a different puzzle. As he was taking us around the cowboy on the horse, we knew that he was thinking about next year's quest and its ultimate solution. We reckon the maize maze obsession of Adrian Fisher gives him new opportunities for creative expression every year, and is a joyous way to turn Old Father Time's scythe to good use 🌱

MAIZE MAZE PATHFINDERS
(OPPOSITE) PUZZLING OUT
A MOST ANCIENT LANDSCAPE
CONUNDRUM, WITH A SAFE-
RETURN DEVICE – CLOTH ON
BAMBOO STICK.
GARDENS OF THE GREATEST
NINETEENTH-CENTURY BRITISH
PALACE, WITLEY COURT; IT HAS
A TWENTY-FIRST-CENTURY
ADJUNCT (RIGHT), A BRONZE
FROM THE JERWOOD SCULPTURE
PARK FOR CONTEMPORARY
WORKS IN THE GROUNDS.

Witley Court
GREAT WITLEY, WORCESTERSHIRE

'Flying shafts of silvery splendour fall upon the fountain. Softly the Triton mourns, as if sobbing below his breath, alone in the moon-enchanted fairyland of a deserted garden.'
Sir George Sitwell, *On the Making of Gardens* (1909)

At Witley Court, the hand of time the great destroyer is all too apparent. It was once considered the greatest nineteenth-century palace in Great Britain, with 50 main rooms, and 50 more below stairs, all heated by 30 tons of coal per day. There were 100 servants, 25 gamekeepers and 10,000 hectares (25,000 acres) of land. Now it is a burnt-out shell. Its story is one of large family fortunes being made, spent, and finally going up in smoke, but the whole scenario spans nearly four centuries and has taken much longer to play out than that British catchphrase for making and losing a fortune, 'clogs to clogs in three generations'.

The renovation and enlargement of Witley Court can be traced through two families who both made their money in the West Midlands of England. The first of these were the Foleys, who prospered in the late sixteenth century by making nails. In the next generation, Thomas Foley increased the family fortunes through the manufacture of cannons and other armaments, and bought Witley Court in 1655. The medieval house was removed and an imposing Jacobean house built in its place. This in its turn was refaced in cut stone in the eighteenth century, to become a fine Georgian mansion.

At the beginning of the nineteenth century the then Lord Foley married the daughter of the Duke of Leinster and commissioned John Nash to make substantial improvements to the house, which included the addition of a very impressive portico on the south wing. These extravagances were too much, and the house was

sold to William Ward, the first Earl of Dudley, who had become one of the richest men in England through those essentials of the Industrial Revolution, coal, iron, limestone and fireclay. His wealth meant the house could now be doubled in size. William Nesfield, who has been called the leading nineteenth-century designer of parterres, was employed to design the very extensive formal gardens, shadows of which still remain. Inspired by the gardens of sixteenth- and early seventeenth-century France, such as Fontainebleau, the Tuileries and Marie de Medici's formal gardens at the Luxembourg Palace, he made a princely garden worthy of this Victorian palace.

This was the high point of Witley Court's fortunes. The Dudleys in their turn ran out of money at the beginning of the twentieth century, and in 1920 the property was sold to Sir Herbert Smith, known as 'Piggy' for all the obvious reasons. He had the pretensions to live in a

great house but not the money. When a fire destroyed one wing of the house on 7th September 1937, there was insufficient insurance money to pay for its restoration, and it fell into decay.

For almost forty years nothing happened, except that in 1954 the house was bought by an antique dealer who sold virtually any and all decoration or ornament or building material that was worth something as reclamation. There were various plans to tear it down, remove the chapel to London, or turn the gardens into a race track. None of these came to fruition and the Department of the Environment took over responsibility for the building and its surrounding landscape in 1972. Since 1984 it has been maintained by English Heritage.

Today, the visitor to Witley Court is amazed by its grandeur. With only the outer walls remaining, together with its pillars, porticoes and window surrounds, the house looks like the perfect palace for any Sleeping Beauty. After walking through the roofless great hall to the Nash portico, the first thing that meets the eye on looking out over the Nesfield gardens is the vast oval pool, which contains what is reputed to be the largest fountain in Europe. It is called Perseus and Andromeda, after the major statues in the centre of this enormous eye-catcher. Today, there is only a shallow depth of water in the pool but when it was first designed it was part of an enor-mously elaborate water system which produced a main jet that rose almost 36m (120ft) into the air, surrounded by a series of smaller jets. The whole system was both gravity-fed and engine-driven. It was said that the rumble of the water coming towards the fountain was as loud as an express train: so loud that the ground truly trembled and conversation stopped.

This fountain is in the centre of a vast open area, on ground which falls gently away from the house and then rises gradually to a great semicircle where there is a wall and a ha-ha dividing the garden from the land-scape beyond. Nesfield planned very elaborate parterres in the squared areas around the fountain and pool, but these have all disappeared, except that the impressive ghostly shadows of their patterns can still be seen when the sun is at the right angle. Some distance from the pool, there are two large classical stone gazebos in which people could sit and watch the fountain in all its glory. On the east side of the house, there was a very elaborate parterre at the end of which was a circular pool with a fountain and a statue of the goddess Flora.

On the southern wing of the house is a conservatory, now roofless, which was considered to be one of the wonders of Witley Court. It was similar in size to the magnificent conservatories built thirty years earlier at Chatsworth for the 6th Duke of Devonshire by Sir Joseph Paxton. This enabled the owners to show off their collection of tropical ferns and shrubs.

Below the carriage drive is an area that was once an eighteenth-century wilderness, with rocks, a cascade and a valley garden. This is being restored, and contem-porary sculptures by Antony Gormley, Elizabeth Frink and Lyn Chadwick have already been placed there, as part of the Jerwood Sculpture Park. More will be added, together with a visitors' centre. It is envisioned that people walking through the gardens will move along a ribbon of time that starts with the contemporary, regresses into the ruins of a magnificent house and culminates in the sight of the Victorian fountains in glorious dramatic spate once more, giving the water displays which nobody has seen for sixty years. Landscapes are all about cycles of change over time, and the history of Witley Court encapsulates that story 🌱

THE CENTRAL PERSEUS
FOUNTAIN SCULPTURE
(OPPOSITE), CARVED FROM
A SINGLE BLOCK OF STONE,
IS REPUTED TO BE THE LARGEST
FOUNTAIN IN EUROPE.

GLORIOUS FULL SPATE
OF PERSEUS FOUNTAIN (ABOVE)
SOUNDED LIKE AN EXPRESS
TRAIN WHILE SHOOTING UP
ITS MAGNIFICENT JET TO 36M
(120FT).

form

In reality, landscape design is outdoor sculpture, not to be looked at as an object,

but designed to surround us in a pleasant sense of space relations.

James C. Rose, *Pencil Points* (1938)

The phrase 'space relations' from Rose's essay is one of the clues to all garden and landscape design. Space governs the form of the garden, and it is experienced through the spatial relationship between the ground plane (or horizontal form) and the raised elements (the vertical forms). A further factor will be the harmony or contrast between these horizontal and vertical forms and the space beyond the garden or landscape boundary. Any idea that a garden designer may have, from whatever source – allegorical, historical, architectural, sensual, or inspired by existing features in the garden or landscape – is expressed through the garden's form.

Frank Lloyd Wright, the greatest American architect of the twentieth century, has eloquently and wonderfully summed up our idea on form: 'Ideas exist for us alone by form . . . the artist's work was thus a revelation of the life-principle which shall make our social living beautiful because organically true.'

Form in the garden or landscape is a broad and complex subject. We have tackled it with designs that stress form by emphasising the inward- or outward-looking use of space in relation to the ground plane. Form may also be expressed through variations on those most basic techniques at a designer's command: opening or closing and screening or framing. These techniques can be used to guide the observer or lead the visitor, often subconsciously, to and through the form in the garden or landscape. Form is elemental to how a garden is planned and used.

Everyone has different priorities for their gardens, and one of the first considerations in planning a garden is to decide on its function. Is it to be for entertaining; for looking at from indoors; a plant obsessive's patch for growing treasured specimen plants; aspiring to be a piece of art; inward-looking and surrounded by an enclosure; or outward-looking, bringing the surrounding country into the garden through orchestrated viewing points? Each of these various types of garden will dictate a different form when considered in relation to the designated plot.

A garden's natural form will affect its design. A very steep slope almost invariably involves building terraces and steps, while a flat area can be quite dull. A small change of level in a garden, even if it is only one step down or up, makes it both visually and physically more exciting. The garden's main aspect, whether north, south, east or west, is an important factor to consider (and providing protection from the prevailing wind can sometimes be even more important). It may be difficult to change the natural form of a small town garden and there will be little need to create vistas through to the borrowed landscape. However, in the countryside the borrowed landscape may be of considerable importance, so that the garden is planned to take advantage of this natural asset, with paths or vistas being placed so as to lead towards views near, medium and far in the surrounding landscape.

A barren dramatic escarpment of red sandstone on his estate inspired an eighteenth-century aristocrat, newly returned from the Grand Tour of Switzerland, Germany and Italy, to create a romantic landscape, reminiscent of his travels. At Hawkstone Park in Shropshire, Sir Rowland Hill directed the visitor on a winding pathway about 5km (3 miles) long to find grottoes, follies and a classical column, all part of his imaginary journey to various places around the world. Pines and firs were planted on this natural formation in the landscape so the surrounding views would only be visible as and when Sir Rowland intended. From the top of the column, The Monument, thirteen counties can be seen on one of those unusual clear days, yet while in the wood it is difficult to know whether to go left, right or straight on. Sir Rowland and his son, Sir Richard, both played with form in a humorous way, enjoying tantalising visitors with views of steep drops from the escarpment.

Sometimes the treatment of the surrounding landscape, through control of the space, can come as a great surprise. At Hidcote Manor in Gloucestershire, Lawrence Johnston made a garden on the edge of the escarpment, with a staggering view of the countryside below which he then proceeded to camouflage. Visitors to Hidcote usually remember a series of garden rooms, and yet there is a long vista only a short distance from the house, leading to iron gates that apparently open to infinity. The form of the garden only becomes apparent on reaching the gates and looking through them to the hidden view, stretching into the far distance towards the Brecon Beacons in Wales. Johnston was a genius in designing gardens and this vista is one of his crowning achievements.

Form can be entirely manmade, given sufficient resources and expertise. The biggest single span glasshouse in Europe has recently been built in Carmarthenshire, in south Wales, where it emerges from the side of a very gentle hill. Kathryn Gustafson has dug a wide path down into the centre of the glasshouse, eventually reaching a depth of 5m (16ft), thereby establishing another horizon and greatly increasing the apparent height of the structure. Then, a series of paths leads to the different plant zones. She has deliberately juggled with the visitor's sense of direction, so that the voyage of exploration within this manmade form is quite different from the one that anybody might be expecting.

Two contemporary, but quite different, approaches can be found near and in London. The Lyceum, in the Essex garden of Stephen Anderton's family house, is a formal reflection of light, focal point and stage, using classical rectilinear shapes to give an immediate formality to the garden. In high contrast is the biomorphic, sinuous-shaped pool in the centre of the courtyard at the Lexington, a revamped block of flats in the City of London. The pool and the free-form planting beds were inspired by the great twentieth-century Brazilian landscape designer, Roberto Burle Marx, and their shapes work wonderfully as a counterpoint to the severe Modernist 1960s flats and other buildings enclosing the courtyard space.

There is something in mankind that makes us want to change that small bit of the world which we may call our own. Sometimes change may be necessary for practical reasons, such as protection from the wind, or next door neighbour, but sometimes it is just part of a wish to be different. The longer that we design gardens the more we are concerned with the natural landscape that either is or was there and that its contours and formation are used where possible in designing another space. As Daniel Kiley has remarked, 'Man *is* Nature. When we shape the land, we are Nature too. But we must be attuned to the systems of Nature.' Slowly we are educating our clients to feel more content with what Nature has provided. After all, she has been very imaginative in supplying an almost endless variety of forms in our gardens and, just as the wisest advice about what to plant is 'what grows on yonder hillside', so the best advice for the shape or structure of your garden is to look at and respect its initial form

ADJACENT CIRCLES IN THREE
DIFFERENT FORMS AT SHILL HOUSE
(PREVIOUS PAGE).

THE MONUMENT, 1795 (RIGHT) IN HONOUR OF SIR ROWLAND HILL, THE FIRST EIGHTEENTH-CENTURY 'IMPROVER' OF HAWKSTONE HALL. THE COLUMN OF THE TUSCAN ORDER IN SANDSTONE IS 30M (100FT) TALL.

THE RUSTIC OAK SWISS BRIDGE (OPPOSITE) OVER THE CLEFT WHICH DR SAMUEL JOHNSON, IN DRAMATIC LATE EIGHTEENTH-CENTURY LANDSCAPE TERMS, DESCRIBED AS 'THE SUBLIME, THE DREADFUL, AND THE VAST'.

Hawkstone Park

WESTON-UNDER-REDCASTLE, SHROPSHIRE

'This place has great rude [i.e. wild] beauties and the owner is continually improving it. The rocks are more frequent and wild than at Studley Royal and the prospect more extensive and various.'
Phillip Yorke, a visitor to Hawkstone Park (1748)

The 360 hectare (900 acre) park at Hawkstone is not far from Shrewsbury, in a comparatively flat area of Shropshire. Within the park, two dramatic red sandstone outcrops or escarpments emerge from the surrounding plain. The larger rises precipitously to a height of 37–55m (120–180ft) and is about 800m (½ mile) long. It is bounded by two large, manmade pieces of water, the Menagerie Pool on one side and Hawk Lake on the other. A long, wide valley divides the main outcrop from the smaller one, which is 25m (80ft) high by about 400m (¼ mile) long. Traditionally, the smaller escarpment has mythic connections with the Arthurian legend and the

battle between two giants, called Tarquin and Tarquinus, both of the Red Castle. The remains of this thirteenth-century medieval castle, which had an inner bailey surrounded by a wall, still stand on the escarpment.

Hawkstone was bought by the Hill family in 1556. Two centuries later, one of the succeeding heirs, Sir Rowland Hill, started transforming the natural sandstone escarpments into one of the most amazing Picturesque walks to be made in England in the late eighteenth century. He placed follies and garden features from far-flung but fashionable inspirations as disparate as ancient Greece and Rome, medieval England, Italy, Switzerland and Corsica along the escarpments. The placing and height of the various follies control the way the escarpments are looked at (by drawing the eye) and the way they are looked from (by providing viewpoints for the fantastic views over the plain and the Hills' surrounding land).

The Hill family's magical creation persuaded people to follow a route or circuit. This was very much an eighteenth-century garden design fashion, as the gardens by Lancelot 'Capability' Brown testify. Sir Rowland's idea was that the visitor would be on the equivalent of a magical mystery tour: discovering its mysteries would need both determination and courage (although the Hills were thoughtful enough to provide a guidebook in 1783). Nowadays, it could even be thought of as an upmarket prototype for a Disneyland experience, with its miniaturisation of foreign travel.

When Sir Rowland Hill began making the circuit in the 1750s, there were very few trees on the escarpment, so all his follies would have been clearly visible while walking along the Grand Valley between the two escarpments. An urn marks the start of the adventure, at the top of the large escarpment. It was placed there by Sir Richard Hill in the 1790s, in memory of his father, Sir Rowland. From here the circuit goes to the White Tower, an octagonal building built, despite its name, of red brick that may once have had a lime wash. Steps lead

up to a very fine mid-eighteenth-century sitting room with a fireplace which is thought to have been filled with medieval armour and banners at one time.

A little further on is the Roman-inspired Monument, which was erected by Sir Richard Hill in 1795 as an ostentatious eye-catcher, intended to impress everyone who saw it with the family's wealth and power. The classical white sandstone column of the Tuscan order, 30m (100ft) high, has a circular internal staircase of 152 steps. Forever embellishing the top is a statue of Sir Rowland. It is said that on a fair day thirteen counties

can be seen from the narrow, balustraded viewing balcony just below the statue, and the visitor is very aware of the far hills of Wales beyond the great plain in which the escarpment stands. When the Monument was built, the Hill incumbent could truly say he was lord of all he surveyed, because the Hills owned most of the surrounding land.

The path winds through trees to a place where a Swiss bridge made of wood crosses a deep gulf in the escarpment, known as the Cleft. While taking the tortuous paths along the large escarpment between the White Tower and the Cleft, the visitor would once have seen breathtaking views of the rich farmlands in the surrounding countryside. Today, these are barely visible through the trees that Sir Rowland planted, but are being opened up again as part of a restoration programme. The bridge offers another viewpoint of the surrounding countryside and an excellent view of the Red Castle. It was made at a time when people went on the Grand Tour and sometimes returned frightened and 'awed' by the views they had seen in the high Alps in Switzerland. After visiting Hawkstone in 1774, Dr Johnson remarked on 'its prospects, the awfulness of its shades, the horrors of its precipices, the verdure of its hollows and the loftiness of its rock . . . above is inaccessible altitude, below is horrible profundity.' (In consequence, the ravine over which the bridge is built became known as the Awful Precipice.) When we visited in 2001, the Swiss bridge was extremely unstable, and almost as frightening as Dr Johnson described.

After crossing the Cleft, the path rises up to the grottoes. These may originally have been Roman copper mines, as traces of malachite and other copper deposits can still be found in the walls today. The grottoes are reached by a dark corridor, about 60m (200ft) long, that is awe-inspiring even today, or through a larger entrance into the cliff face, above which a very fine reproduction of a medieval arch was built. In the eighteenth century, fissures in the walls held stained-glass windows representing moments of history, to entertain

the visitors. From here, Reynard's Walk leads down through the woods below the large escarpment and so to the greenhouse and the pleasures of the more conventional landscape.

So many people wanted to come and see the follies (there was much more garden visiting in eighteenth-century England than we recognise) that the family built the Hawkstone Inn, where people could stay while deciding whether or not they agreed with Dr Samuel Johnson's descriptions. Today, the Hills are long gone, and the estate has been sold off. There have been many owners of this dramatic landscape in the last 150 years, and the landscape immediately below the escarpment has changed: it now contains two golf courses, and the Hawkstone Inn has become a very large hotel.

Miraculously, most of the follies on the escarpments, both outward- and inward-looking, have survived. The park is now in the process of a final restoration, which includes clearing many trees and the invasive ponticum rhododendrons that had made it almost impossible to 'progress the circuit' of this magical eighteenth-century garden of follies and views. Hawkstone is truly the making of garden form in the landscape: the form created by nature has been gloriously transmuted by the whims and eccentricities of the Hill family ☙

THE HERMITAGE, WITH ITS THATCHED ROOF (OPPOSITE), MAY HAVE HOUSED A LIVE HERMIT, ANOTHER, BUT OFTEN SHORT-LIVED, AFFECTATION OF EIGHTEENTH-CENTURY LANDOWNERS; HERMITS OFTEN FLED OUT OF BOREDON TO THE LOCAL PUB.

THE GRAND VALLEY IN THE FOREGROUND (ABOVE) FROM HAWKSTONE PARK PRECIPICES, AND BEYOND, SUPERB VIEWS OF SHROPSHIRE AND ON THE FEW VERY CLEAREST DAYS SOME TWELVE OTHER COUNTIES.

BATHING POOL GARDEN

(RIGHT) AND ITS SUPERB YEW

HEDGE PEDIMENT. THE LOWEST

PART OF THE HEDGE IS

BOXWOOD AS INFILL AND

CONTRAST – AN ITALIAN DESIGN

IDEA.

ONE OF TWO FABULOUS

PANORAMIC VIEWS (OPPOSITE)

FROM HIDCOTE ESCARPMENT

OVER THE COUNTY OF

GLOUCESTERSHIRE AND TO

WALES BEYOND, BOTH FRAMED

BY A *CLAIR-VOYÉE* OF PRETTY

ROCOCO ARCH AND GATES.

Hidcote Manor
CHIPPING CAMPDEN, GLOUCESTERSHIRE
Lawrence Johnston

'And in Gloucestershire Lawrence Johnston started to make the garden that, more than any other in England, has influenced the way we garden today.'
Anna Pavord, *Hidcote Manor Garden Guidebook*

One of the great gardens that Hidcote influenced is that other iconic garden we all know and love: Sissinghurst. Both have formal bones and informal planting, and this form became the twentieth-century up-date on their original garden design source, the Arts and Crafts movement.

Lawrence Johnston bought about 120 hectares (300 acres) of farmland on a plateau in the northern part of Gloucestershire in 1907. He was a member of a well-heeled American family, the Whitneys, and this allowed him to spend most of his life concentrating on his obsession with gardens and plants. Though he was unmarried, he was not an entirely free agent as his mother, Gertrude Winthrop, lived with him until she died in the mid-1930s. She was both a guiding light and a restraining hand, since she held the purse strings. (When she died, she left her son the interest on trusts but no access to the capital, much to his disappointment.)

At Hidcote, the land rises almost 91m (300ft) above the surrounding area and has amazing views over the landscape. Johnston was a cultivated man and knew the major gardens in Italy and France very well. Most of these gardens include long, grand vistas, often extending to the perimeters of the estates in which they were made. Yet, partly because of the wind factor and possibly because he was a somewhat introverted character, he and his mother started making enclosed areas around the house. There are now approximately fifteen garden rooms, usually surrounded by yew hedges, each with its own personality.

MEDITERRANEAN PLANTS IN THE ITALIAN GARDEN (LEFT). FAMOUS HIDCOTE TOPIARY YEW BIRDS AND HEDGES (BELOW) WHEN FIRST PLANTED BY LEGENDARY AMERICAN GARDEN DESIGNER. HIS HIDCOTE GARDEN DESIGN WAS THE MODEL FOR HAROLD NICOLSON AND VITA SACKVILLE-WEST AT SISSINGHURST. ENCHANTING PERENNIAL PLANTS IN ONE OF MANY GARDEN ENCLOSURES (OPPOSITE) CREATED BY JOHNSTON FOR HIDCOTE GARDENS, MAINLY TO SHELTER HIS PLANTINGS.

The garden nearest the house is known as the Old Garden, and leads to a lawn known as the Lilac Circle, thence to the Fuchsia Garden, the Bathing Pool Garden (now merely ornamental), and under a yew archway into another circular space with a simple lawn. The Circle is also the beginning of a major enclosed vista that goes past the famous Red Borders and up a set of wide steps, between a pair of matching seventeenth-century-style gazebos, and into the Stilt Garden, where a series of hornbeams have been topiarised into regimented rectangles of greenery. The vista terminates with a view through a gate, or *clair-voyée*, and over the borrowed

landscape beyond: the farmlands of the Vale of Evesham in the foreground, with the Brecon Beacon mountains in Wales beyond.

After serving as a soldier during the First World War, Lawrence Johnston developed a different vision of the gardens at Hidcote. The first thing he did was to create the Theatre Lawn. This is a very large space, which could be used for theatrical events, enclosed by a clipped yew hedge, with steps leading up to a circular raised level at one end. It is an area of great tranquillity, and there is something magical about finding this space unexpectedly, after the movement and intricacy of the garden rooms.

At about this time his mother started to have less influence over Lawrence Johnston, although there is a garden room called Mrs Winthrop's Garden, planted with a selection of the Mediterranean plants (including some very spiky ones . . .) with which Johnston became fascinated when he bought another property, called Serre de la Madone, near Menton in the south of France. This was to become his main home from the 1930s until he died in 1958, although he returned to Hidcote during the war.

His last grand gesture at Hidcote was to make the Long Walk which can be glimpsed from one of the gazebos. It is a very wide grass walk, hedged with yew, with areas that are heavily planted with trees on either side. (One of them is known as Westonbirt, and the others are called the Pine Circle and the Stream Garden.) Visitors feel impelled to stroll up the Long Walk, towards the gate which can be glimpsed at the end. The gate or *clair-voyée* appears to open into the sky beyond, but when visitors reach it they are amazed to see the most wonderful view over the landscape of three counties, spread out beautifully below.

This is a fine example of Johnston's wonderfully imaginative use of space and form. Most people would have been tempted to design the garden so as to reveal the surrounding landscape, but here it is hidden until the two gates are reached. Only then does it become apparent that the garden is set high on a hillside, and that there are meadows far below where sheep may safely graze. There is even a hidden ha-ha, so that the sheep may not graze too closely to the protected paradise Lawrence Johnston made for himself on his piece of hill in Gloucestershire

SIDE VIEW (RIGHT) OF
UNIQUE AND VERY SPLENDID
EIGHTEENTH-CENTURY
EARTHWORK AMPHITHEATRE,
THE CENTREPIECE OF
CLAREMONT LANDSCAPE
GARDENS IN SURREY. SEE ALSO
PHOTOGRAPH ON PAGES 2–3.

Claremont Landscape Gardens
ESHER, SURREY

[The Duke of Newcastle] never tired of Claremont, declaring to his wife, '. . . how well Claremont agreed with me that my Friends must come to see me here, and I hope to believe they will.'
Sophie Chessum, *Apollo* magazine (April 2001)

The playwright and architect of Castle Howard in Yorkshire, Sir John Vanbrugh (1664–1726), bought Claremont in 1709, built a house and started designing the landscape. In 1714, the Earl of Clare, soon to be the Duke of Newcastle and the richest man in England at that time, bought the estate from Vanbrugh and renamed it Claremont. He lived there until his death in 1768, by which time he had spent all his fortune.

The Duke of Newcastle was besotted with gardens and landscapes. He and his wife 'doted on "dear Claremont" and its plants and animals as if they were their children. Newcastle worried constantly about the weather and its effect on the garden: too much rain, too little rain, too hot or too cold. He took to heart the death of every tree or the munching of a single evergreen by a wilful sheep' (*ibid*). Soon after he bought the estate he employed Charles Bridgeman, who became its sole landscape designer in the early 1720s. Influenced by the earliest ideas of the Picturesque, the Duke of Newcastle wanted a more informal landscape than Vanbrugh had designed. He was also interested in impressing his friends. So he asked Bridgeman to design an amphitheatre for him, as the final surprise when his guests were making the grand tour of his garden, following the circuit that Bridgeman had laid out.

Bridgeman made the amphitheatre on a hill which sloped down to a flattish area where the edge of the estate was bounded by the old Portsmouth Road. From the road, the ragged and unwashed *hoi polloi* could look across the formal lake that Bridgeman made at the

bottom of the hill, and up to his most impressive creation for the Duke (which became known as Bridgeman's Hill; it is commonly described as an amphitheatre, but there are no records that it was ever used for theatrical purposes). The amphitheatre is a double set of semicircular grass terraces cut into the hillside. It is about 30m (100ft) wide and 45m (150ft) deep. The design might have been based on the Belvedere Courtyard of the Vatican, where there is a great double staircase, designed c.1505 by Donato Bramante and shown in Serlio's *Tutte l'Opera d'Architettura et Prospettiva*.

In 1730, soon after the amphitheatre was built, the poet James Thomson was moved to write admiringly, in his splendid poem *The Seasons*, of 'Clermont's terrassed height, and/Esher's groves, where is/the sweetest solitude, embraced/by the soft windings . . .'. Thomson was one of Lord Burlington's circle, Burlington being the great disseminator of Palladian architecture in the first half of the eighteenth century. The most well-known member of the circle was William Kent, who drew the engravings for *The Seasons*. Kent worked at Claremont after Bridgeman, building a grotto and making his formal lake irregular in shape. The lake can also be admired from a temple building called Belisle, which was designed by William Kent and restored some twenty-five years ago.

When Clive of India bought the property in 1778, he wanted greater privacy and an even more Picturesque landscape than the Duke of Newcastle had created. He arranged for the Portsmouth Road to be moved from the edge of the property to a position approximately 30m (100ft) north where the present road now runs, allowing more privacy, and employed Lancelot Brown. He made the circular lake even more naturalistic in form, and repositioned its obelisk on what appears to be a natural island. Clive of India did not like the amphitheatre and had it planted out with trees and rhododendrons, leaving only a viewing platform at the top overlooking the lake and the Picturesque landscape which Lancelot Brown had created for him.

The amphitheatre became completely overgrown during the nineteenth century, when the house was owned by the Royal Family and was lived in by Princess Charlotte and her husband, Prince Leopold of the Belgians, until her death in 1817. It was subsequently used on an occasional basis by Queen Victoria and Prince Albert and their descendants until 1922. The estate was then broken up and the house (with the north-eastern part of the estate) became a school. The remaining land was sold to a Samuel Rowbotham and was eventually given to the National Trust in 1949, in lieu of death duties. Very little happened for the next twenty years, but in 1975 a generous donation by the Slater Foundation meant that part of the gardens could be restored as they had been originally envisaged by Bridgeman.

For the first time in more than two hundred years, the trees and shrubs were removed from the amphitheatre, its great concentric semicircles of grass were restored and once again 'Capability' Brown's naturalistic lake could be seen from the viewing platform. Although the amphitheatre looks green for most of the year when viewed from the lake, people who walk up to the central terrace realise that in places it is not as perfect as the Duke might have liked, although not for want of trying. It needs regular irrigation, which is not always possible, but the grass is fertilised by hand every spring, and scarified and re-sown in early autumn. Although the angle of the slopes makes cutting the grass quite difficult, this is done every two weeks during the summer by two men using a Swiss machine specially designed for such terrain.

Much of the circuit through the landscape still remains, including the part of Bridgeman's walk that leads towards the icehouse, together with the walk around the lower slopes of the wooded area and around the lake itself. The transformation in the last twenty-five years has been amazing, and visitors now have a much better idea of what a very fine and unique early eighteenth-century landscape would have looked like ❦

CIRCLES ARE MAGICAL. JANE OWEN, BRILLIANT GARDEN DESIGNER AND GARDEN WRITER, HAS BEDECKED (RIGHT) HER CONTEMPORARY OXFORDSHIRE GARDEN WITH SILK BANNER SCULPTURES.

EARTHWORKS ARE A MOST ANCIENT AND CONTEMPORARY LANDSCAPE FORM. BEAUTIFULLY SCALED FAMILY GARDEN WITH PRIMEVAL GRASS MOUND (OPPOSITE) CONTRASTS WITH OWEN'S GARDEN 'ROOM' TO END ALL GARDEN 'ROOMS', ALREADY!

Shill House
ALVESCOT, OXFORDSHIRE
Jane Owen

'One of the alluring features of gardens is their ephemerality. In my garden this quality applies to structure as much to flowers, leaves and seed heads.'
Jane Owen on Shill House

When Jane Owen came to Shill House in 1997, there was nothing in the back garden except for some spring bulbs, some climbers, a few shrubs and a jumble of brambles and thistles over a hump of rubble where a swimming pool had once been. She was not daunted. Jane Owen has designed, looked at and written about loved gardens for more than twenty years, but she hates the British obsession with planting. She thinks gardens should be fun (one of her books, *Eccentric Gardens* (1990), describes gardens of the obsessional and self-taught); however, it is no fun when obsession is taken too far, and gardening is reduced to a competition for producing the rarest, brightest flower,

the greenest lawn or the biggest vegetable marrow.

Jane Owen spent a long time thinking about what she wanted, and knew that it was to do with using circles as expressions of her femininity. Since she had done a design course with John Brookes, she made some sketches. Slowly the plan emerged. The whole garden is to do with the interplay of circles and arcs of circles, used both horizontally and vertically. In the centre there was to be a pool and, very importantly, the line between the top of the water and the edge of the grass was to be seamless. The inevitable question then arose: what to do with the spoil dug out from the pool? The answer was that it would become a mound representing the remaining breast of an Amazon warrior.

A local farmer dug the pool in two days, using his JCB, but it took a further eight months of moulding and stamping before the resulting mound was sufficiently firm to be covered in turf. Jane Owen did this moulding

and stamping herself until one day the grass was laid and the most significant shape in her garden was there. It has changed over its first three years: though the shape has stayed the same, the mound is a great deal lower than when it was first constructed. Liposuction had naught to do with its reduction . . .

Inspired by her children, a humped outer circle defines the whole space. Jane Owen describes it as the serpent or dragon that slips between the house and the garden. This circle welcomes spring with a crown of snowdrops. Later on there are irises. It is never without colour and when the irises are gone she uses artificial freesias made of exquisite blue silk which bedizened the dragon on the day we visited. Apart from a few trees at the back, there are almost no other plants, but Jane Owen wishes the land to be kept immaculate, so her local helper mows the circle, the breast and the crescent every week throughout the summer.

The crescent is another raised area of earth, to the side of the pool. It encloses a semicircle of concrete, large enough for a table and chairs, which is backed by a curved semicircular wall painted a warm cream. Jane Owen calls this the garden room, and says, 'It has been taken to its logical end by adding rugs, standard lamps and portraits . . . this room comes and goes in much the same way as *Alice in Wonderland*'s Cheshire Cat. It also celebrates the whole concept of the traditional garden room which has been hijacked by the twentieth century.' This is a wonderfully surreal addition to the garden.

An archway leads from the garden to a much larger meadow, where Jane Owen has played with circles once again. There is a large circular mown area, in the middle of which is a 3m (10ft) high classical Italianate urn, filled to the brim with water. A pair of plastic ducks float in the urn, which is described as the aerial duck pond. The trees give shade and her two children can play to their hearts' content

THE CLIMAX OF KATHRYN GUSTAFSON'S SPLENDID DESIGN (RIGHT) IS A SHALLOW POOL AND SEEPING STONE WALLS – REFERENCES TO WATER IN ARID OR DESERT LANDSCAPES. THE POOL IS 5M (16FT) BELOW GROUND LEVEL.

GUSTAFSON'S SUPERB CUTTING DOWN INTO EARTH BELOW THE GLASSHOUSE (OPPOSITE) INCREASES THE HEIGHT AND EXTENDS THE HORIZON LINE. PLANTS ARE DISPLAYED MORE INNOVATIVELY THAN IN TRADITIONAL NINETEENTH-CENTURY BOTANIC GARDENS.

National Botanic Garden of Wales

CARMARTHENSHIRE, WALES

Kathryn Gustafson

'I work from the ground. From the contact with the ground I try to evolve emotions.'

Kathryn Gustafson on The National Botanic Garden of Wales

The National Botanic Garden of Wales is the first botanical garden to be created in the UK in over two hundred years. There was once a house called Middleton Hall on the estate, designed in the late eighteenth century by a Sir William Paxton. He surrounded his house with lakes, cascades and dams. The ground plan of the house is still there, and from its site there are amazing views into other parts of Carmarthenshire.

Just below the site of the house is the largest single-span glasshouse in the world. The single shallow glass dome, 95m (310ft) long and 55m (180ft) wide, was designed by Sir Norman Foster and Partners at a total cost of £43 million, half of which came from the Millennium Commission. This amazing construction was intended to display the vast range of plants that are indigenous to the hot, dry regions of the Mediterranean, parts of South Africa, south-western Australia, California, the Canary Islands and Chile. (Twenty per cent of all known species of plant originate from the areas around the Mediterranean, although these cover only 1.7 per cent of the world's surface.)

Kathryn Gustafson, an American and a major international landscape designer, with offices in Seattle, Paris and London, was given the problem of creating a landscape context in which to grow and display the full range of plants from those climates and habitats (which are mainly dry and arid, but are also found next to the sea, on hillsides and occasionally quite high up mountains) so that visitors could immediately see which plants and shrubs grow naturally in which environments.

After an initial site meeting with her partners and

collaborators, Kathryn Gustafson starts by playing around with the basic words that describe the givens of the project. The next stage is making a model, on which she sketches her instincts and intuitions about the ground plan. The Botanic Garden was sketched in Seattle and the rubber mould was shipped to London so a pristine white cast could be taken. The plaster models have tremendous force, for the early decisions seem to have been literally 'cast in stone', and this suits her uncompromising approach. The model becomes a fixed reference point for all the decisions leading up to the project's completion.

During the creative process Kathryn Gustafson realised that she wanted to have as large a planting area as possible, and that she needed to make the design exciting, rather than the serial display of labelled plants that is the conventional and nineteenth-century approach to plant display in botanic gardens. The idea of digging down below the horizontal ground plane came in an intuitive flash, and the main axis of the garden is now a path sloping down 5m (16ft) below the surface, climaxing in a pool enclosed by high walls, as if in a canyon, sculpted subtly with smooth and textured natural stone facings. She had 2,000 cu m (70,000 cu ft) of soil removed and used elsewhere in the landscape, and the path down to the rift valley now greets every visitor as they arrive at the entrance to the glasshouse. Kathryn Gustafson says, 'I love moving masses of earth. But I also love things that have function.' Here, she has increased the space within the glasshouse at a stroke, by lowering the horizon line.

Another of her brilliant design strokes is the narrow, shallow stream of water parallel to the path down into the rift valley. This is the opening beat of her design, and the start of the exploration of the Mediterranean experience at the bottom. As visitors approach the base, they

hear the sound of water and see ahead of them the stone canyon walls, down which water gently falls into a large desert pool. This area is almost as minimal as a Rothko painting.

There are two paths towards the higher levels, one leading to an area where very arid plants grow, and another to an area where the conditions are less extreme. There is also a space for plants that survive fires, as happens naturally in a dry landscape; the keepers of the gardens are working out how to re-create this natural phenomenon. Elsewhere, there is a north-facing cliff, a south-facing cliff, a stream, a lake, rocky levels and boulder-strewn plains. The whole space is large enough for every visitor to take a different circuit through this artificial environment, and they can easily find the plants that they particularly like.

It is too early to be certain how the very wide range of plant material will grow. At present, drought-resistant plants are very close to plants that need a certain amount of water, and only time will tell how well they will live side by side. But after only a year, some of the plants and trees are growing very well, and in a few years' time part of it will look like a forest and part like the barren hillsides that are so often seen in the areas around the Mediterranean.

Everyone is overwhelmed and interested by the voyage they take through the glasshouse. It is already attracting far more people than the directors ever imagined, and most people spend a couple of hours there, when the average time for looking at grounds and landscapes is rarely more than half an hour. It is set to become the major tourist attraction in a part of Wales that has slumbered for many centuries. The combination of Kathryn Gustafson's imagination and tremendous insight as a landscape designer, and Ivor Stoke's knowledge of plants (he is the horticultural director of the gardens) has created something totally unique ❦

ENTRANCE PATH (OPPOSITE) UP THE SLOPE TO NATIONAL BOTANIC GARDEN OF WALES, THE WORLD'S LARGEST SINGLE-SPAN GLASSHOUSE. THE SPIRAL DESIGN FOREGROUND IS OVERWROUGHT BUT THE SERPENTINE RILL WINDING DOWN THE HILL IS ELEGANT.

STEPHEN ANDERTON HAS A SPLENDID DESIGN MADNESS: THE GOLDEN SECTION, HIS BASIS FOR DESIGN (RIGHT) FOR THE GARDEN FOCAL POINT, A GRANITE BAS-RELIEF FABRICATED IN CHINA.

The Lyceum
NEWPORT, ESSEX
Stephen Anderton

'Modernism never got anywhere in this country. It arrived through Europe and flitted straight across to America, and what bit we got in . . . architecture did get itself a bad name very quickly, and we got locked into decoration. Before you knew it we were into Vita Sackville-West and fuss, Rosemary Verey, decorative stuff, and Modernism in gardens never caught on. The Lyceum is about space and proportion and planes and volume.'

Stephen Anderton on The Lyceum

Stephen Anderton is a gardener, a gardening writer and a performer. He was brought up in a minor stately home in Yorkshire, was briefly at the National Youth Theatre, and studied Drama at Birmingham University. He then did a post-graduate course in Landscape Design at Birmingham Polytechnic and became involved in gardening for major estates in the north of England. He finally became the first National Gardens Manager for English Heritage and since the mid-1990s has had a Saturday column in *The Times*. Stephen Anderton claims that he is not a garden designer, but his knowledge of gardens is extensive and his concern with shape and space has enabled him to create an extraordinary garden.

He and his wife and their three children moved to their current home, an early Edwardian house, to find a lot of leylandii, a few dying apple trees and one large shapeless yew. The front door of the house is in a direct line with the garden door, which leads to a terrace – and at the bottom of the garden there is now a beautifully proportioned stage: the Lyceum.

The design is based on the Golden Section, which is the ancient mathematical definition of a proportion that is often used intuitively by artists and architects. It is based on an aesthetically pleasing ratio of about one

ANOTHER GRANITE FOCAL
POINT SCULPTURE (LEFT) ON A
TRANSVERSE AXIS IN THE
ANDERTON FAMILY GARDEN IN
ESSEX.

THE EXCELLENT LYCEUM
(OPPOSITE) AT THE BOTTOM OF
THE GARDEN – FOCAL POINT
AND LIGHT REFLECTOR. BASED
ON THE GOLDEN SECTION AND
THE GREAT BEN NICHOLSON
BAS-RELIEF, DRAWN BY
CHRISTOPHER BRADLEY-HOLE.

third to two thirds. Such was the importance of this concept that it was the basis of all the houses designed by Andrea Palladio in the sixteenth century, after he rediscovered the writings on proportion by the Roman architect, Vitruvius. Palladio had an enormous effect on grand houses built in Europe during the seventeenth and eighteenth centuries, and his superbly proportioned architecture was brought to England by Lord Burlington in the early eighteenth century. But it was the ancient Greeks who originally evolved the Golden Section, sometimes called the Aristotelian Proportion, and Stephen Anderton calls his stage the Lyceum because it was in an Athenian garden of the same name that Aristotle taught his students (and that particular space was used both for teaching and for exercise).

For Stephen Anderton, his Lyceum is part of a historical fantasy. As he says, 'It was designed according to the Golden Section and I rather liked the idea of the Aristotelian Proportion. So there was the stage of Aristotelian proportions. We couldn't lay on golden oiled youths, but we got the girls playing football in front of it, so it was a Lyceum in all sorts of senses.'

Although Stephen Anderton knew he wanted a stage, he felt he lacked the technical expertise to realise his idea. He had been much impressed by Christopher Bradley-Hole's *Latin Garden* at the Chelsea Flower Show in 1998, so he asked him to design the stage. It stretches across most of the width of the 9m (30ft) garden and is about 4m (14ft) high, but the stage itself is only about 2m (6ft) deep. It is made of untreated cedar planking which has now turned grey, and the background is in a soft shade of yellow because the garden faces east and Stephen Anderton wanted a pleasant glow at the end of his garden; the yellow acts as a 'reflector' in the late afternoon when the sun is setting.

When discussing the design of the stage with Christopher Bradley-Hole, Stephen Anderton was influenced by his memory of Ben Nicholson's simple Modernist granite bas-relief at Sutton Place in Surrey, where Sir Geoffrey Jellicoe placed it as a focal point to the large reflecting pool (the last an earlier design by Gertrude Jekyll). This influence is apparent in the final form of the stage.

To one side, the shapeless yew has been clipped into an enormous round ball, and beneath it in the grass are a series of small round clipped box balls which mimic the shape of the yew, but will never be the same size. These shapes remind Stephen Anderton of the glacial boulders deposited in the area in which he lives during the last Ice Age. At one end of the terrace, near the house, another Golden Section sculpture has recently arrived. It was made in China, of textured granite, and its invisible frame cost rather more than the sculpture itself, but Stephen Anderton wanted it to appear to float just above the ground.

There are trees around the Lyceum, and the changes in their shadows as the sun moves across the sky are almost as compelling as an actual performance. Everything in the garden changes with the sun and clouds, or the time of day or night. The lights of the Lyceum can always be lit if there is an audience, and there is a small seating area for the family and guests to sit and imagine what activity will next take place. The structure provides an endstop, focal point and giant eye-catcher in the garden.

Reactions to the Lyceum are mixed. As Stephen Anderton says, 'Some people say it looks like a nasty swimming pool from the 1930s, wouldn't have it given, certainly wouldn't buy the house. But I think Modernism like this has a huge place in gardens.' We agree

GLORIOUS AERIAL VIEW
(RIGHT) OF COURTYARD OF
REVAMPED BLOCK OF FLATS ON
THE EDGE OF THE CITY OF
LONDON. ITS SERPENTINE
DESIGN WAS MUCH INFLUENCED
BY THE GREAT BRAZILIAN
GARDEN DESIGNER, ROBERTO
BURLE MARX.
ROBERT MYERS, THE DESIGNER
OF THE LEXINGTON
COURTYARD, COUNTERPOINTED
(OPPOSITE) THE WHITE
CONCRETE BIOMORPHIC DESIGN
WITH CONTASTING DENSE
PLANTING OF SEVERAL
DRAMATIC LEAF SHAPES.

The Lexington

CITY ROAD, CITY OF LONDON

Robert Myers

'We wanted to design something with a sort of energy and joy to it that had a free form.'
Robert Myers on The Lexington

In the 1960s an office block was built in the middle of the City of London; in the 1990s the building was stripped back to its frame and rebuilt to create a series of high-quality flats called the Lexington. It was designed for people who wanted to live as close to their work as possible. There is a curve on the roof of Old Street underground station, which is near by, so there is a curve on the roof of the redesigned Lexington, and this same curve inspired Robert Myers (of Elizabeth Banks Associates) when he was deciding what sort of garden should be in its courtyard.

Interestingly in terms of urban context, the courtyard backs on to a very old City cemetery, Bunhill Fields, which contains some London plane trees and is adja-

cent to the 2 hectare (5 acre) parade ground that belongs to the Honourable Artillery Company, so there is a nearby sequence of small, middling and large spaces close to the epicentre of the City of London.

When considering what sort of garden design would fit well in the courtyard there were several constraints. There are garages below the courtyard, so it was only possible to have 50cm (20in) depth of soil, and the garden needed to be at a slight angle, so that the irrigation and, more importantly, the drainage would all run into one drainage pipe. Although the courtyard was to be admired from ground level, it would be looked at from above for the most part – and one block of flats goes up eight floors.

The main design is influenced by the great Brazilian landscape and garden designer, Roberto Burle Marx, who was responsible for the wonderfully serpentine walkway in Rio de Janeiro, Copacabana. He loved using sinuous shapes and plant and shrub material that came from the wild. These free-form shapes are very much in evidence at the Lexington, both in the pool and in the irregular areas for planting. The pool surround has a generous raised side with a coping and was designed for sitting, but does not solve the tenants' need for seats with backs, namely: chairs . . .

It was expected that people would stroll through the courtyard, but there are no designated seating areas. Nor is there any bright colour. Both issues have latterly caused some discussion amongst the tenants and the managing committee. Even on the day we were there, Myers was helping decide what seats to recommend, where they should be placed, and how more colour could be introduced into the courtyard. Currently, brightest red geraniums are planted at the edge of the courtyard. Will they finally creep in on a permanent basis? Why is it that clients always interfere with the perfect design?

Much of the plant material chosen is evergreen and some of it is Mediterranean or temperate, such as phormiums and yuccas. There are even a few fashion-able grasses, but not too many, because the designers did not want to have the 'brown look of winter' for a long period of the year. As Robert Myers says, 'We wanted to give it that Burle Marx-type of jungly approach: lots of textures, lots of interesting contrasts of form.'

The courtyard was only finished in 1999, but already the plants and shrubs seem quite at home in the middle of the City. Some wire netting and tall posts make an attractive screen in keeping with the design, and partially mask an unreconstructed 1960s office block. It was hoped this would be a green curtain, but the ever-green honeysuckle has not yet grown sufficiently to be an effective camouflage. The lighting beaming down from two great posts allows the display to be enjoyed when it is dark.

When the water glistens in the pool, the fountain plays, and the plants momentarily remind the viewer of the Mediterranean, it becomes apparent that the designer has embraced the constraints of a small area and enhanced it with a combination of creativity and contemporary materials ❦

materials

Sympathetic modern design, imaginative, of good workmanship and
making skilful use of local materials, is in every case better
than the reproduction of an ancient example, how admirable so-ever.
Gertrude Jekyll, *Home and Garden* (1900)

CONCRETE WALLS, CONCRETE
BONDED-GLASS SQUARES, SLIDE
PROJECTORS (PREVIOUS PAGE)
ARE ALL EXCELLENT
CONTEMPORARY ELEMENTS IN
THIS WONDERFUL DESIGN BY
DIARMUID GAVIN.

PHOTO GRAPHICS, ONE OF
THE NEWEST CONTEMPORARY
ELEMENTS, APPLIED TO GARDEN
SEATS (RIGHT) BY LEADING-EDGE
DESIGNERS, TINDALE AND
BATSTONE.

Traditionally, the materials used in a garden or landscape were those that were most easily available. There is an amazing diversity of materials in the gardens all over Great Britain. In areas where there was very little stone, brick would be used. In areas where stone was abundant, it would be collected from yonder hillside or local quarries. Today, the choice of materials is more complicated because breeze blocks and cement and reconstituted paving are available everywhere. The English have always had a passion for lawns, but we advise clients who have town gardens that such a patch is far more trouble than it is worth, and that they should consider paving, gravel, decking or even astroturf instead, indulging their passion for flowers and shrubs by having many pots or other pretty containers.

Whatever the material, it may be necessary to employ somebody else's talent and skills to install it. This possibility must be faced by those of us who are not technically skilled, because building work in a garden needs to be done properly, otherwise paths crack, walls split, earth spills, water runs, people fall and accidents happen and at the worst the garden may become a danger zone that nobody wishes to enter.

Plants, trees and shrubs are usually the most visible part of every garden, but as landscape designers we know that they are only a part. The hard landscaping is equally important because it forms the structure of the garden. Before a single plant is put into any garden that we design, the initial mantra is drainage, drainage, drainage. Almost inevitably it is nonexistent or malfunctioning, and this has to be corrected before anything else can be done. Foundations for paths, driveways, terraces, walls, ponds or any other architectural elements have to be made, and water and electrical systems installed. Only when the hard work has been done – the paths laid, the walls built, the terraces paved and the ponds dug – can our thoughts turn to the plants that are going to be used in the garden. These preliminary operations take time, skill and money, but aesthetically the most important decisions are about the garden's materials for the basics.

The materials used for paths, walls and paving should be in harmony with one another. This does not mean they have to be of the same material, but it does mean that their colours meld together or are chosen deliberately for their contrast. At Hestercombe in Somerset, the great British architect Sir Edwin Lutyens used Morte slate, which was found just beneath his feet in the garden, and golden Ham stone that came from quarries near by. Used together in this garden, they make a splendidly contrasting combination of colour and texture.

Traditional materials still have a place in contemporary gardens, but materials not usually associated with garden landscapes are now coming to the fore. In the United States, 'Topher Delaney made walls of stainless steel for someone who was obsessed with the contemporary, and we have just finished building a series of glass brick walls in a beautiful arc spanning the garden for a couple who want a glimmer by day and a gentle luminosity at night.

Exciting materials and more sophisticated lighting devices are now available to garden designers in abundance. Fibre optic lighting is increasingly found in the garden because it is high intensity and low voltage. Neon is an inexpensive but dramatic creature of the twentieth century that has travelled from signs and billboards via museum installations and into the garden. Glass technology has made great advances over the past few decades and can be supplied in myriad forms and types (including glass gravel). Fibreglass is a tough, weather-resistant material which is found more and more in contemporary gardens. It is being used for walls and fences, and to make completely natural-looking stones and boulders. Plastics and polymers, used for fencing, paving, sculpture and garden furniture, are also gaining popularity.

Concrete is a material both ancient and modern: ancient because it was used by the Romans, and modern because concrete in various finishes and myriad colours is becoming a much-used element in all kinds of garden landscaping. In a unique garden in Northampton, concrete has been used for the walls of a very special enclosed play area for an autistic child; and in east London, coloured concrete walls and shallow concrete pools form the centrepiece of an amazing sunken courtyard.

Remember, your garden is for you, and it is there to make you happy and content. The more plant material you use, the more time you will spend in the garden, each day and each week, but with the correct choice of stable hard materials you could easily construct a space which gives you immense enjoyment but allows you much more time to sit and contemplate your very own twenty-first-century hard-edge Garden of Eden ❧

THE TURNING POINT OF THE
GARDEN FROM WHICH ALL
PATHS LEAD (RIGHT).
PERGOLA COLUMNS
(OPPOSITE) ALTERNATE CIRCLES
AND SQUARES OF LOCAL
STONE, MORTE SLATE, CUT THIN
AND STACKED, SHOWING SIR
EDWIN LUTYENS' METICULOUS
ATTENTION TO ARCHITECTURAL
DETAILS.

THE MAGNIFICENT SUNKEN
GRAND PLAT AT HESTERCOMBE,
SOMERSET (OVERLEAF),
CONSIDERED AN APOGEE OF
THE ARCHITECT/GARDEN
DESIGNER COLLABORATION OF
GERTRUDE JEKYLL AND EDWIN
LUTYENS.

Hestercombe

TAUNTON, SOMERSET
Sir Edwin Lutyens and Gertrude Jekyll

Hestercombe is remarkable for the bold concise pattern of its layout, and for the minute attention to detail everywhere to be seen in the variety and imaginative handling of contrasting materials, whether cobble, tile, flint, or thinly coursed local stone. In the design details of steps, pools, walls, paving or seating, Lutyens is seen here at his best.

The Oxford Companion to Gardens (1986)

Hestercombe estate is first mentioned in an Anglo-Saxon Charter of 854 and from 1391 to 1872 was owned by the Warre family. In the late eighteenth century, the wonderfully named Copplestone Warre Bampfylde, who had married the Warre heiress, designed and laid out a splendid Picturesque garden on the hills, in the valley and around a lake behind the house.

In 1872, the estate was bought by the Portman family

and in 1904 the Hon. Edward Portman asked Edwin Lutyens and his garden design collaborator, Gertrude Jekyll, to lay out the gardens on the south side of the house, overlooking Taunton Vale and the hills beyond. Almost all the landscape seen from that view belonged to the owners of Hestercombe until 1944. Like the Hills at Hawkstone, they were lords of all they surveyed.

Edwin Lutyens and Gertrude Jekyll had collaborated on projects for about fifteen years by the time they started designing for the Portmans. At the beginning of the work, Luytens was 35 years old, and Jekyll was 61. Their partnership created some of the most important houses and gardens in Great Britain in the early part of the twentieth century, and the project at Hestercombe was undertaken when the designing duo were at the height of their powers.

The ground at Hestercombe sloped away from the house, so Lutyens constructed a series of terraces which

led down into a square, sunken garden, known as the Great Plat, 38m (125ft) square. (There were considerable technical difficulties with the design, for streams run through the property, and the area needs more drainage than was actually incorporated; some elements of the stone landscaping rest on rather uncertain foundations.) The entire area that Lutyens designed sits on strata of Morte slate, which is a very dark grey form, and this was used wherever possible for creating the walls and many of the decorative elements of the design. Sometimes his detailing required a stone that could be carved more delicately, and he chose the golden Ham stone, which came from quarries only 25km (15 miles) away. To emphasise some of the designs of the pavements he chose local flint and his signature tile-on-edge. Miss Jekyll suggested that old millstones could be effective in the centre of circles, and they are.

The way Lutyens used and detailed materials in his designs was always superb. Sometimes on the horizontal the Morte slate became paving stones, but in the hemispherical pools flanking the entrance to the Great Plat the slate has been used in a much more imaginative way. Thin slate slabs are set on-edge in semicircles in the walls, with keystone fountain masks, echoing shallow-pooled seventeenth-century Italian garden grottoes but set down in Somerset.

Lutyens was very clear about the way he wanted both the family and their visitors to explore his space. The terrace close to the house most conveniently leads to an area called the Rotunda (a wonderful example of Lutyens' use of materials) from which there are two routes, either eastwards towards the Dutch Garden, or to balustrading and steps into the lower areas of the garden, centred on the Great Plat. Two long, narrow rills of water, edged with Morte slate, flow through grass terraces on either side of the Great Plat. The rills are fed

ROTUNDA GARDEN (LEFT)
MOST EXQUISITELY 'DRAWN' BY
EDWIN LUTYENS AND MADE OF
TWO TYPES OF LOCAL STONE:
HAM STONE AND MORTE SLATE.
GETRUDE JEKYLL'S DUTCH
GARDEN DESIGN (OPPOSITE) AT
HESTERCOMBE HAS A
ROLLICKING GENEROUS
PLANTING WITH ONE OF HER
SIGNATURE EDGING PLANTS,
GREY LAMB'S EARS.

from the pools below the balustrade of the upper terrace, and lead to the pergola on the far side of the sunken garden. The pergola's columns (brilliantly alternating between square and round) are made of thin-cut stacked Morte slate, supporting wooden beams, and the entire structure provides a spectacular frame for the view of the distant landscape to the south. A circuit of the Great Plat can be made along a path at the same level as the pergola or by entering the Plat itself down six semicircular steps at each corner. There is a stone sundial in the centre, and one of the gardeners suggested that the whole garden is a sundial and that the feature in the middle is in fact the gnomon.

On returning to the Rotunda and turning left, the Orangery comes into view. It was used to protect orange trees during the winter and as a place for entertaining, but it is now empty. Inside, in the middle of the main wall, there is a magnificent Lutyens-designed fireplace made of black slate, with great swags of fruit and leaves carved out of Ham stone on either side. There are similar swags on the outside of the building and the walls themselves are a mixture of dark Morte slate and golden Ham stone.

Some steps lead up to the Dutch Garden, a formal parterre divided by Ham stone pathways. The beds have always been planted with lamb's ear, catmint and lavender, one of the simplest and most effective plant designs

THE PLANTS GERTRUDE JEKYLL USED WERE CHOSEN FOR THE SCULPTURAL FORMS THEY MAKE AS THEY COME INTO MATURITY IN MID TO LATE SUMMER.

ever devised by Miss Jekyll. Her planting plans for the design were found in a potting shed at Hestercombe, where they had been stuffed into a drawer and lain

undisturbed for nearly seventy years. Further research found a second set of plans at the University of California, Berkeley, in the United States, and more information has become available recently.

These plans were essential when the Somerset County Council, who own Hestercombe and had leased it to the Somerset Fire Brigade as their headquarters, decided to restore this Lutyens and Jekyll collaboration. There has been considerable simplification of the plant material used in the Great Plat compared with that originally replanted in the early 1970s, and the planting is now closer to the original plans. The plants Gertrude Jekyll used were chosen for the sculptural forms they make as they come into maturity in mid to late summer. She was also aware of the need for contrasting textures of leaves and flowers. Against the high stone wall that divides the garden side of the house from the Great Plat, she used grey- and silver-leaved plants, because many of

these plants originate in the Mediterranean and are drought-resistant, making them particularly suitable for areas which receive a great deal of sun. These have been replanted here. But some things have changed: the borders designed by Henry Hall in 1878, immediately in front of the house above the Great Plat, have been planted again as formal parterres, with bedding plants that would have been used in high Victorian bedding schemes.

The gardens at Hestercombe are not only about materials changeable, such as plants, and materials unchangeable, such as stone, but also about time. The eighteenth-century Picturesque landscape, only restored in the last few years, the formal lines of exuberant colour from the late nineteenth century, and the subtleties of an early twentieth-century garden, restored in the last two decades of that century, are each expressions of their unique time in the history of gardens ❦

THE GREAT DANISH DESIGNER
ARNE JACOBSEN CHOSE A
RECTANGULAR DESIGN MODULE
AND VARIATIONS (RIGHT) FOR
ALL MAIN ELEMENTS IN THE
ARCHITECTURE AND GARDENS
OF ST CATHERINE'S COLLEGE,
OXFORD.

A LONG CANAL LEADS TO THE
MAIN ENTRANCE (OVERLEAF)
AND REFLECTS A BARBARA
HEPWORTH STATUE.

St Catherine's College

OXFORD

Arne Jacobsen

'The only reason why Oxford University approached Jacobsen was because a feisty member of the sub-committee responsible for the construction of its new college happened to be crazy about mid-50s Danish design. A posse of dons was dispatched on a whistle-stop architour of Denmark. They trooped around buildings by Fisker, Hansen, Moller and Utzon (the last architect of amazing Sydney Opera House) but it was Arne Jacobsen's schools, houses and his half-finished headquarters for Scandinavian Airlines that blew them away.'
Wallpaper magazine (1998)

St Catherine's College is one of the newest colleges at Oxford and was built in the 1960s by a great Danish architect and designer, Arne Jacobsen. He was influenced by the International Modernism of Bauhaus and the *Weissenhofsiedlung* or 'white house estate' (Germany's bid to replace the dark and squalid public housing from the past) which had buildings by some of the greatest of his contemporary twentieth-century architects: van der Rohe, Gropius and Le Corbusier.

The college trustees had been highly impressed by the materials Arne Jacobsen used and by his incredible attention to detail, but the British architectural community was disappointed with the choice of a foreigner. One angry architect, in best Little Englander style, said that it was the worst insult to British architecture since the eleventh century when a Frenchman had rebuilt Canterbury Cathedral.

The college and its grounds are on an island between two arms of the River Cherwell that had been used for many years as a rubbish dump. The buildings border the playing fields of Merton College and are on a site where there had been allotments, so the college now appears to be in a rural setting. The main access is across a somewhat formalised tributary of the River Cherwell which is 3m (10ft) wide. Various water plants, including rushes, grow in the margins of the waterway, and a fine sculpture by Dame Barbara Hepworth is sited on one of the several paved terraces at the edge of the water. The entrance to the college buildings immediately parallel to the formal water is screened by two lines of beech hedging, the second staggered behind the first, so that there are effectively three *allées* of beech obscuring the back gardens of the terrace houses on the other side of the river.

Jacobsen conceived his Oxford college buildings and gardens as a series of modules, which stretched 3m (10ft) from north to south and 2.5m (8ft) from east to west. This module was standardised for everything throughout the new college, so that the overall plan is extremely geometric. The materials for both the gardens and the buildings are predominantly brick and pre-cast concrete. In the gardens, Jacobsen had originally hoped to use York stone paving but that was too expensive, so he had to settle for concrete paviours instead. The concrete was coloured to a tone that he specified. The bricks are standard yellow bricks rather than the handmade ones that he had originally designated, which also proved too expensive. The third material he used is yew, in the form of a series of oblong hedges, 3m (10ft) long and 2m (6ft) high, which divide the buildings and the various gardens from one another.

ONE ANGRY ARCHITECT, IN BEST LITTLE ENGLANDER STYLE, SAID THAT IT WAS THE WORST INSULT TO BRITISH ARCHITECTURE SINCE THE ELEVENTH CENTURY WHEN A FRENCHMAN HAD REBUILT CANTERBURY CATHEDRAL.

The yews have now grown to full size and make an excellent contrast with the textures of the brick, concrete, glass and steel in the buildings. Everything is rectilinear, with the exception of a very large circular grass lawn immediately in front of the Provost's Lodge, on which there is now a large cedar. Jacobsen originally specified a cedar of Lebanon at least 9m (30ft) high, and one was found, moved, planted, and died a year later. Another tree was found and planted and is now at the height Jacobsen wanted but it is not a cedar of Lebanon and does not have the horizontal branches that he liked. Eighteen months ago a small cedar of Lebanon was planted; in thirty years' time it may replace the cedar that is currently there and thus finally fulfil Jacobsen's ideal of allowing a single, particular tree within the strict symmetry of the architecture.

Jacobsen was also asked to design the college furniture (much mistreated original examples of his most famous and endlessly copied chair, the 3107, are in the common rooms), door handles, ashtrays, cutlery and even condiment sets, making what our German cousins would call a *gesamtkunstwerk* (a complete artwork). As *The Oxford Companion to Gardens* (1986) remarks, 'Jacobsen abhorred the word "inspiration", maintaining that a good design was only achieved through hard work on the drawing board.' He saw no point in colour, and when summer annuals were planted he commented, 'It looks like a dog cemetery'. For him, colour in the landscape was supplied by the muted tones of the materials used in the buildings and the different shades of green in the gardens, which strictly maintained the completeness of his artistic vision.

Today, the guide to the gardens of St Catherine's College lists more than two hundred different types of shrub and climber. These include roses, which Jacobsen hated, but in general his vision has been kept almost exactly as he intended. A landscape which depended only on space, form and materials was revolutionary at the time he conceived it, and even forty years later the combination of these elements, dictated by a master, continues to create admiration for twentieth-century college architecture's first modern classic ☙

DRAMATIC WATER FEATURE

(RIGHT) WITH A SINGLE
CONCRETE RECTANGLE AS BOTH
DESIGN AND BRIDGE IN A
CARDIFF GARDEN BY TINDALE
AND BATSTONE.

FORMAL BUT MODERNIST
CONCRETE GATE PIERS
(OPPOSITE) AND BEAUTIFULLY
SCALED, GENEROUS STEPS FOR
ACCESS TO GARDEN.

Three Gardens by Tindale & Batstone

CARDIFF AND LONDON

Helen Tindale and Karena Batstone

Guy Cooper: What particularly persuaded you both that contemporary materials were needed in gardens now?

Karena Batstone: We felt limited by the old traditional materials such as brick and York stone paving that we had been trained to use. We were interested in concrete, and in extending the use of interior materials outside, and surprised more designers weren't using glass, steel, plastic and, say, polycarbonate instead of glass, for it's stronger and lighter.

Helen Tindale and Karena Batstone met in 1991, at the English Gardening School at the Chelsea Physic Garden which is organised by Rosemary Alexander. Helen Tindale then went to the United States and worked for Oehme and van Sweden in Washington DC for a couple of years before returning to London. Meanwhile, Karena Batstone had been teach-

ing design at the English Gardening School and had written a book called *A Handbook for Garden Designers* (1994). In 1994 they met again and formed their partnership. Though they live in different towns (one of them in London and the other in Bristol), they find that working at a distance by fax and e-mail is not difficult because they have very similar views about garden design.

At the gardening school they were taught to use traditional materials such as brick and stone, but they now prefer to use concrete and low-cost industrial materials that are usually employed inside a house, including glass and sheet plastic (and they have found that polycarbonate makes a good substitute for glass, as it is lightweight, much less expensive and doesn't break and splinter). Their initial problem was to find contractors who were used to installing kitchens and bathrooms and were therefore familiar with metal and

plastic but were also able to adapt their skills to working outside without being brutally careless about trees, shrubs or plants they thought were in their way.

Once they had found suitable contractors, the two designers had to persuade their clients that using these materials would give them spaces that they would like and enjoy, with the added benefit of very low maintenance. These are not quite 'No plant gardens' but the partners acknowledge that plants are of subsidiary importance when considering the design and its implementation. They also agree that one of the most influential source books for their designs was our award-winning book on contemporary gardens, *Paradise Transformed: The Private Garden for the Twenty-First Century* (1995). (We just had to mention it!)

In a private garden in Cardiff, Wales, the clients were very keen to keep some existing fruit trees and they also wanted a lawn where their children could play football.

Outside the back door, the designers made a very large terrace of polished concrete, on which stand three large square galvanised containers filled with herbs. These were the only plants allowed. Three grass steps, the full width of the terrace, lead down to the garden, where irregularly shaped pathways made of wood, with a galvanised finish on each edge, lead through the existing fruit trees. These are underlit with fibre optics, so they make a star walk at night. Remembering her Washington experience, Helen Tindale planted tall grasses beside the walkways to enhance and slightly conceal the areas on either side.

Another Cardiff garden also has a large concrete terrace but it has been left in its natural colours to harmonise with the gravel areas. There is a large reflecting pool, partly inspired by Mondrian's pupil, Jean Gorin, with a series of stepping stones. The pool is very shallow, because the owners have five children and the garden

THE EXQUISITE AESTHETIC OF CONTEMPORARY SIMPLICITY: THE LOW RAISED BOARD WALK (LEFT) TRANSFORMS THIS TRADITIONAL BACK GARDEN.

BOARDWALK FIBRE OPTIC LIGHTING (BELOW) IS A SUPERB AND SIMPLE ADDITION TO ANY GARDEN, WHETHER CONTEMPORARY OR TRADITIONAL, FOR IT NOT ONLY ILLUMINATES BUT ALSO HAS MYRIAD AESTHETIC POSSIBILITIES.

TINDALE AND BATSTONE ARE TWO OF THE MOST INNOVATIVE YOUNGER BRITISH GARDEN AND LANDSCAPE DESIGNERS. (OPPOSITE) THEY HAVE USED STUNNING PHOTOPRINT-COVERED PLANT CONTAINERS.

needs to be as safe as possible. It, too, is lit by fibre optics so that the garden is interesting by day and night.

For Helen Tindale and Karena Batstone, the most significant trend in garden design is the erosion of the division between inside and outside, so that the two spaces become as closely connected as the British climate will allow, with similar use of styling, materials and colour in both areas. Since people have less and less time to spend in their gardens, they want a space where they can relax and the children can play, somebody can cook and everybody can laze. Because of this, minimum maintenance is always uppermost in their minds. Karena Batstone has strong opinions on garden maintenance. Clients usually ask for a low-maintenance garden, and she is happy to comply. As she says, 'I for one hate gardening. I have enough housework to do without having to do the garden as well. The plants we choose are selected for their self-sufficiency' (so the Beth

Chatto approach to plants is alive and well with younger designers as well).

The designers say, 'Groovy gardens are asymmetrical and dynamic, inviting movement around a space with level changes bridged with slides (not just for kids) and ramps to increase accessibility and play value.' These changes of level are vitally important because they move people from one area of the garden to another, taking them on a circuit without their conscious knowledge.

The importance of artificial lighting cannot be exaggerated. Each piece of lighting is appropriate to the area

of the garden, being shadowed or spotlit, and they like the owners to be able to control the lighting as they wish. The lighting may take the form of colour wash, fibre optic trees or images from projectors, which are chosen by the owners and can be changed according to their whim. (One of their ideas is to project images of jungles between swaying plantings of bamboo – offering two different garden realities.)

WE FELT LIMITED BY THE OLD TRADITIONAL MATERIALS SUCH AS BRICK AND YORK STONE PAVING THAT WE HAD BEEN TRAINED TO USE.

In Helen Tindale's own small garden, she plays with the latest materials and techniques that intrigue her. The partners are experimenting with 'glass gravel as substitute for stone gravel, acrylic interior-lit cubes for seating or storage, graphic elements, cubes, digital wallpaper, glow in the dark paint, poetic lines to personalise a space, fake grass, clients' personal images from large-scale projectors (some of their favourites are country plantings, abstract images of their designs and images of nature: flocks of birds, penguins, icebergs, etc), fibre optic *shrubs* and *hoses* coiled as light sources or for skipping . . . weight sensors to trigger lighting, solar-powered light sources, gobos (moving effect projectors) and videos!'

However, cabbage seeds bought two years ago are now growing a third of the way across the concrete paving in Helen Tindale's garden, so a plant may win after all! Nothing is permanent and their ability to cross-fertilise their ideas for the use, choice and shapes of a very diverse range of materials means that their gardens reflect the needs of families in the twenty-first century

WOODHAMS, THE KING OF GALVANIZED GARDEN CONTAINERS, ARE NOW SHIFTING TO COPPER AS A BACKGROUND (RIGHT). PLANT CONTAINERS ON RIGHT ARE STACKED CONCRETE SEWER RINGS.

INSIDE AND OUTSIDE, INTERIOR TO EXTERIOR (OPPOSITE) THE DESIGN – AMAZINGLY AT THE REAR OF A SMALL LONDON TERRACE HOUSE – COORDINATES THESE DESIGN RELATIONSHIPS THROUGH SCALE, SHAPE AND, MAINLY, COLOUR.

Ultra Modern Garden
KENNINGTON, SOUTH LONDON
Stephen Woodhams

'The whole idea behind the space was to be a fusion of the old and the new. I don't think anything you see here is necessarily ground-breakingly new – contemporary is just the use of materials available now – but what I love most is the juxtaposition of not only building materials but unusual plant material too.'

Stephen Woodhams on the Ultra Modern Garden

Stephen Woodhams has had an obsession with flowers ever since he was a small child and he attributes this to the fact that his grandfather had a nursery in Kent. He was also a very young entrepreneur, and at a tender age saved up enough money to buy a greenhouse so that he could sell bedding plants to his teachers. He was lured by Wisley and attended the two-year horticultural course run by the Royal Horticultural Society, and then set up a landscape construction business with two other students, Andrew Farthing and Alistair Jones. A few years later, he left them and opened his first florist shop near Notting Hill Gate. This became very successful and in 1994 he had his first garden at Chelsea Flower Show; it won a Gold Medal. His business has flourished, and the main flower shop is now at No. 1 Aldwych. (Meanwhile, his former partners have gone on to become the principals of an excellent garden contractor firm, Landscapes Unlimited, to which we subcontract all installation of our major design work.)

As well as designing gardens, Stephen Woodhams is also involved in organising parties and functions, and marketing a range of products used in the garden. He became well known for his association with galvanised containers for the garden. He did not originate the idea, but his public relations skills attracted a great deal of personal coverage. Now he is experimenting with copper containers, which are given a special glaze so that they remain copper-coloured and do not develop verdigris.

His own garden in Kennington is typical of south London. It is a long, narrow enclosure, 4m (13ft) wide (the same width as the house) and extending about 9m (30ft) to the back wall. Stephen Woodhams' design notion is one of common currency: the inside (house) should reflect the outside (garden) and vice versa, so the reclaimed concrete flagstones start in the kitchen and flow through the garden to the back wall. The enclosing garden walls have been rendered and painted the same colour as the conservatory, thereby extending the kitchen space into the garden. There are no blinds in the conservatory, because Stephen is quite unworried by the neighbours 'peeking over the garden wall'.

Along one side of the garden there is a series of handsome containers made out of concrete sewer pipes, placed one on top of the other, in which copper beeches have been planted. Stephen Woodhams is fascinated by concrete and he has found an easy way of colouring these containers so that they blend into the overall colour scheme of the garden: they each have neon rings at the base as lighting colour wash. In his experimental copper containers he is growing traditionally clipped box balls.

Like all good florists, he is possessed with an awareness of colour and its contrasts and harmonies. Although his garden is mainly in tones of beige, umber, hot reddish pink and green, he has some deep orange canna lilies which act as a bright contrast focus to the colour range of the garden. The palette of colour in the garden changes with the season. Sometimes the colours will be adjusted for a single night according to the colours of the vegetables or flowers on the dinner party menu: the plants in the containers may be changed to complement the food, with the colours spilling out into the garden in flower arrangements as well.

Even in this small garden, there are different plants or a tiny hidden section of the garden that cannot be seen from the house. Equally, when looking back down the

garden from the back wall, the view into the house is almost as interesting as the view out. Stephen Woodhams never knows what the next contemporary material he uses will be, but at the moment he loves neon. He has recently worked on a penthouse garden, which he made in different shades of blue, adding a long line of blue neon around the stone edging of the wall that protects the garden, to define the enclosure after dark.

Perhaps surprisingly, Stephen Woodhams says that the garden designer who has influenced him most is Sir Geoffrey Jellicoe, and he bemoans the fact that Jellicoe has only become better known since his death. Stephen Woodhams seems 'wired' into what is happening now (as is proved by the expansion of his business activities). When advising about gardens he is very aware of materials, both old and new, but it is his eye for colour, either in plants or materials, that gives an extra edge to his designs

CONTEMPORARY ADDITION

(RIGHT) TO GARDEN OF

GRADE II LISTED NORTHAMPTON

FAMILY HOUSE: CIRCULAR

CONCRETE ENCLOSURE WITH

GLASS BLOCK SQUARES

UNDERLIT WITH FIBRE OPTICS

AND CIRCULAR PORTS FOR

PROJECTING IMAGES ON WALLS.

INCREDIBLY BEAUTIFUL

FLORA (OPPOSITE) FASCINATED

BY LIGHT: DISNEY IMAGES,

CASCADING FIBREOPTIC

STRANDS AND SHINING

THROUGH GLASS BLOCKS IN

THE LAWN.

Flora's Garden

DURNGATE, NORTHAMPTONSHIRE

Diarmuid Gavin

'I get my ideas from everywhere. My experiences are not restricted to gardening ones. I have always been fascinated by design in all its forms, whether that be clothes design, architecture, art or the pop video during its heyday in the 1980s. It's been a fascinating experience exploring the use of some new materials, colours and plants in a more subtle and challenging way: a combination of suburban, traditional and modern.'

Diarmuid Gavin on Flora's Garden

No one could have invented as strange and unlikely a life history as that of Diarmuid Gavin. He was born in the suburbs of Dublin and claims that he was bored by living there; only in retrospect did he realise that it was a safe haven to prepare him for a totally different lifestyle. Having trained in Ireland as a garden designer at the College of Amenity Horticulture at Glasnevin in Dublin, he established his own garden design business there.

He designed a garden for the Chelsea Flower Show in 1995 (and shocked the RHS judge brigade of British gardening's great and good with his use of that revolutionary twentieth-century building material – the glass block) and suddenly became a television star, being best known for his popular *Home Front in the Garden* series with Laurence Llewelyn-Bowen, in which Diarmuid makes the gardens outside the rooms that Laurence transforms, and another series on his own, *Planet Patio*. He says that he has had little influence on contemporary garden design, but we disagree. We think Diarmuid Gavin's television gardens have been at the forefront of the changes taking place in the private garden in Britain (even if we are not in tune aesthetically with some of his designs).

In Northampton he was asked to design a garden for Jim and Katherine Anderson, their teenage son, Kyle, and, most importantly, for their autistic daughter, Flora. The design constraints were complicated, because the house is a listed building of historic interest Grade II, as are the walls in the garden, which means that there are considerable restrictions on any building work. But most importantly, the garden was for Flora and, at eleven years old, she was both startlingly beautiful and very strong. Left to her own devices she ripped up everything in the old garden, every plant, every shrub, and threw stones and pebbles over the walls to devastating effect on the adjacent parked cars, causing many thousands of pounds' worth of damage. So Flora had to be gently but effectively controlled within her garden, where she could touch and enjoy, but not destroy.

The solution is a roofless circular room made of concrete, approximately 4.5m (15ft) in diameter and about 3m (10ft) high. There are two gated entrances into this space, making the enclosure Flora-proof. Once inside she may do whatever she likes. All the plants in this circular garden are in troughs built in round the top of the wall, so she can see the plants, admire them, but not touch them. There is a pattern of glass blocks in the circular paved area, with fibre optics beneath. At night these give a wonderful display of changing colours. Strands of fibre optic lights fall from the top of the wall, and there are two concealed projectors in the walls. At the press of a button, Flora can watch and change a series of images specially selected for her. Many of them are from Disney World, where she has been on several occasions. She loves the carnival colours. Kyle has a different set of images he can play (many of them involve fish, with which he is obsessed). He was surprised by

Diarmuid Gavin and his parents, for they got a local newspaper photographer to take some colourful pictures, and these local references make the images even more exciting for both children.

The water feature – effectively a large stone ball sitting in a very shallow concealed reservoir – was too attractive for Flora, because she would rip off her clothes and bathe using the very small amounts of water to wet herself from top to toe. It is still there, but the water has ceased for the moment.

There is a small terraced area near the house where Flora's parents can sit and relax. From here they can see Flora in her circular enclosure, and even have a quiet barbecue when they wish. All in all, Diarmuid Gavin has come up with a wonderful set of design solutions for the family, using the most modern materials – concrete, glass block, fibre optics and projected images – to create an amazing set of spaces for four different people with different needs. They are all very happy with it, and we have yet to find a more successful, imaginative and contemporary garden in such a small area 🌱

SO CORRECT SOMEHOW,
THE SOFT AND HAIRY HOUSE
(RIGHT) IS IN A JAPANESE NEW
TOWN – TSUKUBA NEW SCIENCE
CITY – AND THE HOUSE IS A
LEADING-EDGE ATTEMPT TO
BLUR AND IMPROVE LINE
BETWEEN HOUSE AND GARDEN.

ANOTHER FINDLAY

ARCHITECTURE ESSAY
INTERRELATING THE STRUCTURE,
(OVERLEAF) THATCHED POOL
HOUSE, WITH PLANTS; NOTE
THE 'GARDEN' ON THE RIDGE.

Thatched Pool House

SOUTHERN ENGLAND

Ushida-Findlay Partnership

'The challenge to all green designers should be the integration of buildings with their contexts as seamless fusions of each other, as syntheses of ecological processes already in place, and as monitors of people's subliminal reactions to environmental signals, which can then be translated into billboards of the collective unconscious. These objectives are the complete opposite of most traditional twentieth-century architecture but they are also the wave of the future.'
James Wines, *Green Architecture* (2000)

Kathryn Findlay grew up in Scotland and trained at the Architectural Association in London, before being awarded a scholarship to Tokyo University. In 1986 she set up an architectural practice with her then husband, Eisaku Ushida, and only returned to Great Britain a couple of years ago, having lived in Japan for almost twenty years. James

Wines has described Kathryn Findlay's work in Japan as being in the forefront of twenty-first-century architectural development.

She integrated almost completely with Japanese culture and this has been an enormous influence on the way she approaches any design project. She says that there is no distinction between fine art and design in Japan; it is all seamless. The art of living, the art of writing, the art of having tea, the art of flower arranging have all become ritualised, and the rituals arise from the way people lead their daily lives. This means that a designer uses all the senses when designing.

This was only part of the story when the Ushida-Findlay Partnership was asked to design a Soft and Hairy House in 1994. The house was to be in Tsukuba New Science City, one of the largest new conurbations created since the Second World War. The received opinion was that Tsukuba was destined to become yet another dreary cxurb and it has, with a few design and architectural exceptions, including Arata Isosaki's amazing Civic Centre, with its deconstructed paving design (he reversed it) from the piazza for Rome's Campodoglio by Michelangelo, and the Soft and Hairy House. Both projects were radical, political and polemical.

The partnership had a telephone call from a couple who had read Salvador Dali's statement that the architecture of the future should be soft and hairy. It was a surreal notion, and from this they created a biomorphic flowing house. Kathryn Findlay says, 'We tried to make a relationship with the existing landscape because we were cutting green fields to build the house, so we actually replaced what was cut by putting it on the roof. It was part of the whole idea that it's a soft form. And it got a soft sort of lining inside the house – it's all lined in fabric. The hairiness comes from the shaggy, hairy, strange, wild planting on the roof.'

The house has very few rectilinear elements and the form flows and rises, quite literally, from the very small landscape in which it is situated. Looking at the house, it is difficult to tell where the green of the field merges into the area covering the roof, in which Findlay has planted dill and other herbs, together with some indigenous plants. There is no break between the architecture of the house and the immediate landscape. The living rooms look out on to an interior courtyard and up to the green and hairy roof. In the courtyard there is a surprise, for emerging from one corner is a vast blue egg with a porthole window which is, in fact, the bathroom. On the roof is a traffic cone, acting as both an eye-catcher and the exhaust hood from the oven in the kitchen below. Nothing is as it seems.

In Great Britain, Kathryn Findlay was approached by someone who wanted to build an enclosed swimming pool in the grounds of his house. Both the house and the wall at the back of what is now the swimming pool are listed as being of historic interest, so a further set of priorities had to come into play with her design. The listed wall (which cannot be changed) is covered with a small stone roof and became part of the inspiration for the idea that the swimming pool roof should be made of thatch. From the garden, the Thatched Pool House looks like a long thatched barn, except that there is a line of small rectangular glass windows where the ridge on a thatched roof would normally be. Immediately outside the glass windows, at the ridge, are lines of plants – irises, cow parsley, reeds, and grasses – growing in concealed planters.

Kathryn Findlay took her inspiration for the planting from Japan. 'When I was designing the thatched roof, I looked at parallel technology in Japan and I discovered that from the Neolithic Age they had actually planted the ridges, and in Japan now, on the thatched roof, you get these ridges of irises and wild flowers and the roots become a binding material to anchor the ridge of thatch.'

Inside, the swimming pool could not be more contemporary. It is Olympic size, with floor-to-roof glass walls on three sides, and the listed wall on the fourth. A lining of waterproof material goes all the way around and up to the ceiling. The interior is part of the twenty-first century and the exterior is a building that is almost timeless: a traditional shape with a most traditional vernacular thatch roof that could be from Great Britain or Japan. The magic is that, when inside looking up to the glass ridges in the roof, gently moving wild plants can be seen growing there, together with the occasional bird feeding from them.

Kathryn Findlay commented: 'At night, which is very nice, you get a very seamless, clean-looking, modern interior with the glimmering pool and the heavy benevolent dark cloud of thatch, and one seems to float above the other. So you get this other sense of garden inspiration which is release and surprise. Surprise is one thing and release is another, and when you see something float you get a sense of release.' With the Thatched Pool House, perhaps the Floating World comes to Great Britain . . .

WATER PATTERN MOSAIC
(RIGHT) OF PALE AND DARK
GREY SETTS IN CONTEMPORARY
SHALLOW POOLS IN A SUNKEN
COLLEGE COURTYARD.

BRILLIANT PLAYING WITH
GARDEN DESIGN PLANES
(OPPOSITE) OF WALL, WATER,
SHEETS OF SLATE AND MOSAICS
UNDER THE WATER BY SUSANNA
HERON; NOTE THE SINGLE
PERFECT BIRCH TREE.

Hackney Community College
SHOREDITCH, EAST LONDON
Susanna Heron

Susanna Heron grew up in Cornwall, where her father Patrick Heron lived for many years. He was one of the most prominent of all the artists who lived in or near St Ives in the middle of the last century, and was so important internationally that the great American artist, Mark Rothko, came to sit at his feet, confirming the theory that Abstract Expressionism originated not in New York City but in some major way in the depths of Cornwall.

Susanna Heron has inherited some of her father's genius but her artistic sensibilities are expressed in sculpture rather than as paintings. She loves working outside, and is very sensitive to the way light changes every day, to the difference in people's mood depending on whether the weather is hot or cold, and to the different materials that she uses to create her sculptures and land forms.

Hackney Community College occupies a site of almost 3 hectares (7 acres) and was begun in the early 1990s. When Susanna Heron became involved with the project the construction of the buildings was already in full swing and the large courtyard was a churned-up area of hardened soil, scattered with the detritus of building. She was told that there was going to be a subterranean library, which would be entered at lower ground level, and was to look out on to an open space at the same level below ground, so that people using the library would see into an enclosed area open to the sky. Opposite the library, in the main quadrangle of the college, a very large London plane tree had somehow survived all the chaos of the new construction around it.

No sooner had she been given the commission than she went to Italy for some weeks and pondered two things: what sort of wall should enclose the area, and what colour was it to be painted? In Lucca she saw the medieval wall around the city, which has a path at its base and a wide battlemented walkway at its top. In Florence she stood in a courtyard and looked up to see the brilliant blue Italian sky, which she described as the 'depthless blue sky of Florence in October'. She also saw another wall in Florence painted a dynamic shade of gold, with foliage at the top. These visual moments remained in her mind and were variously incorporated in her design. She realised that the supporting wall of the Sunken Courtyard should be painted a brilliant blue and should be reflected in water, and that is what was built.

The materials are extremely simple: water, Delabole slate from Cornwall, black and white granite setts, *blanc de bierge* composite paviours, a rendered blue concrete wall and a single stunning birch tree with the whitest of barks, *Betula jacquemontii*. The water feature covers most of the sunken courtyard area, and is made up of two areas, with water falling from one into

the other. There is a rectangle of finely polished slate just below the surface of one pool, and the neighbouring rectangle has a mosaic of wave patterns in black and white granite setts.

At ground level, metal balustrades surround the courtyard so that the students can look into the large reflecting pools. Anyone standing outside the library below can look up to see the top of the people looking down. Both human placements and actions are reminiscent of details found in fifteenth-century Italian frescoes. Looking out through the library windows is like looking into the great courtyard of a grand palazzo, with water in the centre, and the changing light making patterns on the huge blue wall. Suddenly the depressing hole is not depressing any more and the sunken courtyard is now passed and enjoyed by most of the college students every day. People's responses are very different. Susanna Heron has said it is meant to make you feel that

you have time to stand and stare, and the Clerk of Works for the college says that he loves to come here when he arrives in the morning because it makes him feel as though he is sitting on a beach on holiday.

For Susanna Heron, the most important material in her design is water. She says, 'You could look at the water in terms of material, because what you are doing then is looking through the water at something beneath it. You are looking at the substance of the water, which actually is not without colour. And you are looking also at the reflection in the surface, with the granite and the slate just below the surface, which intensifies anything that reflects in it, and the tree and the blue wall reflect in the slate under the water.' She uses a simple spectrum of materials, but her artful manipulation of scale and shape is highly effective. Hers is a fine artistic sense, brought to garden design ☿

water

The brilliant contrast of dancing, refracting jets against trees or shaded buildings
gives the eye the delight that is at the root of impressionism.
A single jet alone, in suitable settings – where there is a dark background for choice –
has the beauty of some miraculous flower.

Gertrude Jekyll, *Garden Ornament* (1927)

The thing about water is that it can do what nothing else can do.

Daniel Kiley

TEMPLE OF PIETY (PREVIOUS PAGE) REFLECTED BEAUTIFULLY IN SECTIONS OF MAJESTIC CRESCENT AND MOON PONDS AT STUDLEY ROYAL, YORKSHIRE, IN SHARP CONTRAST TO WILDWOOD TREES AND SHRUBS IN BACKGROUND. **AT NIGHT** NEON LIGHTS FRAME THE MIRROR (RIGHT) WHICH REFLECTS THE FLOATING PLANTS.

The earliest known gardens are the Paradise Gardens, designed in ancient Persia about 3,000 years ago. Water was an essential feature in these gardens, together with enclosure for privacy and security. The rill, an exquisite narrow ribbon of water, originated in Persia and was later brought to the gardens of Spain by the Moors. It became a primary water feature in Western European gardens, particularly those made in Italy during the Renaissance, and William Kent designed an outstanding example at Rousham Park in Great Britain in the eighteenth century. Water in one form or another has always been used in gardens, both as a necessity and to give pleasure to the eye and ear.

A natural source of water, such as a stream or a river, was originally essential to the creation of water features in the garden. At the Villa d'Este, in Renaissance Italy, the garden-mad cardinal channelled the River Aniene into myriad water displays, with hundreds of jets, falls and rills, and at the splendid Villa Lante, a head of water in a natural stream is fed down through the garden, often piped underground, to emerge as various water features. It runs through the top of a stone banqueting table, and is then configured to form rills, fountains and pools, before flowing down a water slide into four square pools, to climax in jets from the points of a geometric metal star held aloft by four bronze athletes. It disappears into the garden, only to reappear a little further away, outside the enclosure of this marvellous, iconic, sixteenth-century creation, as a focal point in the *bosco* or woodland setting of the villa.

By the end of the seventeenth century, water was being used in imaginative ways on the aristocratic estates of Great Britain, with canals and complex water features playing an important role in landscapes such as Wilton House in Wiltshire. A more naturalistic style of landscape design in the eighteenth century was reflected in a preference for informal, irregularly shaped lakes, placed at some distance from the house to act as major eye-catchers. Supreme examples of such creations can be seen at Stourhead in Wiltshire and Blenheim Palace in Oxfordshire. Formality reached a simple magnificence in the early eighteenth century with the lawn-bounded moon and crescent ponds at Studley Royal in Yorkshire and, of course, the much smaller-scale Mughal-inspired rill in the twentieth century by the great Sir Geoffrey Jellicoe with his low waterfalls descending so beautifully through the grassy sward at Shute House in Dorset.

The invention of machinery that recirculated water meant that water features could be used in smaller gardens where there was unlikely to be a source of natural water. Most British houses were connected to a mains water supply in the late nineteenth and twentieth centuries, and many gardens had a small pond with a few goldfish, at the very least. We always try to persuade clients to include a water feature in their garden, despite the additional maintenance involved. The sight of water adds a sense of peace to the garden and the sound of water helps to disguise other noises impinging on a garden's serenity.

The simplest installation is a jet of water, falling and recirculating through a glazed pot or bowl. A pool will reflect the surrounding garden, the clouds and sky, and the changing patterns of light throughout the day. A water wall, made of stone, glass or metal, can be orchestrated so that the water falls as a smooth sheen that is barely audible, or as a more vigorous waterfall effect, which will also add heightened sound. A small misting unit creates yet another pleasant effect, particularly if it is lit at night. Aluminium sections, shot-blasted or acid-etched glass sheets, rusting steel or stainless-steel sections, old scaffolding poles or parts of oil drums can all be used to create water features that reflect the imagination of the owner and reflect the twenty-first century.

Contemporary water technology becomes more sophisticated every year. We love this description of water play in gardens: 'What pleases me most in these new fountains is the variety of ways with which they guide water, turn it, lead it, break it, make it rise and fall.' The irony is that the statement comes from Claudio Tolomei, a sixteenth-century Italian grandee. He would have been delighted with the new water dance in the Great Courtyard at Somerset House in the centre of London, which can play so many variations on the rise and fall of its water jets, enhanced by patterns of colour at night, controlled by the most sophisticated computerised water system. Good Signor Tolomei would also have been dumbstruck by the ingenious floating and moving metal dishes of plants in the pools in a back garden at Epping in Essex. The technology may develop, but the fascination of water never changes

A RUSTIC AND NATURALISTIC
BRIDGE (RIGHT) ON AN
INFORMAL STRETCH OF THE
RIVER SKELL BELOW FOUNTAINS
ABBEY WHICH BECAME AN EYE-
CATCHER TO THE MAIN VIEW IN
STUDLEY ROYAL WATER DESIGN.

CENTRE OF THE SPECTACULAR
MOON POND (OPPOSITE) SET IN
ITS BEAUTIFULLY CLIPPED GREEN
SWARD AND HEDGES,
EMBRACED BY STEEP, WOODED
HILLSIDES OF RIVER VALLEY.

Fountains Abbey and Studley Royal

RIPON, NORTH YORKSHIRE

The water gardens at Fountains Abbey and Studley Royal are the finest in Britain and probably the most visited of all the landscapes belonging to the National Trust, attracting more than 300,000 people a year. They are now a World Heritage Site. Like all the greatest landscapes in the world, they were the product of one man's obsession. That man was John Aislabie, the Chancellor of the Exchequer in 1720 at the time of the first great financial crash, the South Sea Bubble. He was blamed for the catastrophe, expelled from Parliament, imprisoned, disqualified from public life and retired to Yorkshire where he had inherited an estate called Studley Royal.

Aislabie had taken an interest in the landscape of his estate before the crash, but he became obsessed with it once he retired there. Though he had not been to Italy, he knew both William Kent and Hawksmoor, and would have seen some of the Italianate gardens that

they installed at the beginning of the eighteenth century. Like all good chancellors, he was able to hold on to most of his fortune (our fantasy is that he fled from London in a grand and fast coach, stuffed with bank notes and bullion bars . . .) and he spent some of it altering and taming the route of a small river called the River Skell.

The river is naturalistic while flowing through the ruins of Fountains Abbey, once the greatest monastic foundation in Christendom, and Aislabie's formalising of the river only begins below the ruins, as does his fantastic 'green garden': a large lake, grotto springs, and a long, formal canal adjacent to the fabulous climax of his design, the Moon Ponds: one round, full-moon pond framed by two crescent-moon ponds, set in smooth grass lawns overlooked by the superb Temple of Piety. From the Moon Ponds, the river rushes over a formal, stone-stepped cascade, on either side of which perch

A **PAINTING** (LEFT) OF
FOUNTAINS ABBEY BY
BALTHAZAR NEBOT, 1768.
PHOTOGRAPH BY CLIVE
BOURSNELL IN 2001 BRILLIANTLY
ECHOES THE SAME VIEW OF
FOUNTAINS ABBEY IN NEBOT'S
PAINTING.

two exquisite classical summer pavilions, known as the
Fishing Tabernacles. Having flowed through the 24
hectares (60 acres) of Aislabie's landscape, the Skell
meanders on through more steep wooded banks
towards the town of Ripon.

John Aislabie built several pavilions and summerhouse eye-catchers. Halfway up the hill immediately
opposite the Moon Ponds is the Banqueting House,
designed by Colen Campbell, from which visitors can
look down upon this wonderful formal landscape,
though the trees which have grown up in the last two
hundred years interrupt the present view. Behind and
above the Moon Ponds is another viewing point, the
Octagon Tower, which has recently been restored and
from which the ponds and the lake can both be seen.

A path through the woods leads to the Temple of
Fame, a classical wooden rotunda from which the landscape can be admired once more. Further along the path

is Anne Boleyn's seat, which has also been restored
recently. Here John Aislabie's son, William, provided
another viewing point for Fountains Abbey and for the
towers of Ripon Minster, the other main architectural
eye-catcher near by, which can no longer be seen.

By the time William Aislabie inherited the estate
from his father, there had been a considerable change in
people's taste. Landscapes had become more naturalistic, taking the form of the unique British contribution to
garden history, the Picturesque. William added
Fountains Abbey to the estate in 1767 and altered the
course of the River Skell once more, so that it flowed
over two cascades before joining the first crescent-moon
pond. He wanted the visitor to be surprised by the
sudden view of the ruins of Fountains Abbey, and was
extremely successful in planning a circuit or progress
from the cascades to Fountains Abbey and back. It
remains an incredible journey through woods, classical

elements and water, used both naturally and formally and, most importantly, acting as a mirror to the trees and sky.

There have been changes since William Aislabie died. Studley Royal House, which is some way from the landscape that he and his father created, was burnt down in 1946, and the stable block (not a bad place to store horses, with its grand and beautiful barrel-vault drawing room) designed by Colen Campbell in the 1720s for John Aislabie as his home while the big house was being built, again became the home of the former private owners of Studley Royal House (for whom we completed a complex and beautiful formal garden). That house and the 2 hectares (5 acres) around it are still privately owned, but most of the rest of the estate is now a fabulous deer park in which about 350 deer, including fallow, red and Manchurian sitka, roam freely.

On the whole, the landscape remained untouched because William Aislabie's heirs did not have sufficient money or interest to make radical changes. The National Trust is trying to restore the eye-catchers that have been lost, to clear vistas that have become overgrown and to re-create, as far as possible, the ideas that the two Aislabies had for this incredible site in North Yorkshire. One of the main problems is the unpredictability of the River Skell, which produces too much water at some times, and too little at others. Aislabie had been warned about this by aristocratic friends who were amateur devotees of the fashionable Picturesque 'landskip' style. It is hoped that modern water technology will be able to correct this haphazardness (a large holding control reservoir is one proposed answer) for, without the River Skell, the most amazing eighteenth-century water landscape in Britain would not exist 🌱

EIGHTEENTH-CENTURY
ROMAN-INSPIRED STONE BUSTS
(RIGHT) SET IN ARCHED NICHES
OF THE HIGH BEECH HEDGE
OVERLOOK THE CANAL AT
SHUTE HOUSE.

SIR GEOFFREY JELLICOE'S
BRILLIANT RILL OR CENTRAL
WATER FEATURE (OPPOSITE) AT
SHUTE HOUSE WHERE HE HOPED
TO MIMIC MUGHAL INDIAN
WATER CHUTES, EACH
WATERFALL GIVING A DIFFERENT
MUSICAL NOTE.

Shute House

SHAFTESBURY, DORSET

Sir Geoffrey Jellicoe

'The richness of Shute derives I suppose from the combination of some scholarship, providing that sense of depth, together with the action of the subconscious mind in the design process and the involvement in that way too of the two clients, Anne and Michael Tree.'
Sir Geoffrey Jellicoe on Shute House

When Michael and Lady Anne Tree moved to Shute House in 1970, they invited Sir Geoffrey Jellicoe to redesign the gardens. He was a natural choice, as Michael Tree had known him since the 1930s, when he designed the grand gardens at Ditchley Park for Michael's parents, Ronald and Nancy Tree (the vivacious, amazing American, Nancy Lancaster of Colefax & Fowler fame, who was also a much respected creator of gardens).

The idea that garden design is all about access and exits is seen at its best in these gardens. The house opens directly on to a road and from the front there is no indication at all about the landscape beyond. It is only after going through the house to the garden side that a wide strip of land takes the eye beyond the ha-ha to the beautiful borrowed landscape of the Dorset countryside, framed by mature trees and hedgerows. Shute House stands exactly on the boundary of Wiltshire and Dorset, and the main view from the back of the house is towards a gently rolling hillside with a village and church tower almost hidden in the distance. On the right-hand side there are three informal ponds which lead into one another and so into the landscape. These are balanced on the other side by a larger reflecting pond which is a home for ducks and swallows.

Nobody knows exactly how many springs rise in the gardens, but we were told there are at least thirteen. Most of the water features are fed from one small, but beautiful, natural spring which has been there since

time immemorial. The water seeps silently into a pool and bubbles up gently with extraordinary clarity, since it is filtered through chalk. The pool itself, being quite deep, appears to be a black green with water moss softening the flints. It is thought by the long-term inhabitants of the valley to have magical properties. Its clarity and purity certainly evoke images of holy springs and nymphs venerated by ancient peoples. Jellicoe altered the shape of the pool slightly, but it is so enclosed by the surrounding trees that it becomes a secret fount, reflecting the trees and the dappled light filtering through the leaves.

It was these natural water resources that inspired Sir Geoffrey Jellicoe when he first came to Shute House. The area that he redesigned is to the right of a wide lawn, hidden from view by trees and hedges. At the end of a path is an intriguing gate, but immediately beyond there is only a very dark, enclosed, triangular area with a formal stand of evergreen oaks and a tall beech hedge, with glimmers of light coming through two openings in the hedge. These openings are balustraded in wood by

balconies facing into the formal seventeenth-century-style canal, which was already there when Jellicoe arrived. It was extended in the early 1970s, and finally completed in 1984. About 30m (100ft) long, the canal turns at right angles into the woods to make a more informal, vaguely rectilinear water feature. Towards the house, the ground rises to a backdrop of an even taller yew hedge. Set into niches in the hedge are Roman-inspired classical busts on plinths, standing above stepped box terraces. On the side of the canal opposite the hedges there are lilies in pots, and a path beside them leads further into the woods.

To the left of the darkened triangular area, the remains of a very formal potager, made up of six large squares of box hedging, are visible through the hedge. A gap in the hedge leads to an amazing water feature and the centrepiece of Sir Geoffrey Jellicoe's design. This is a rill with a series of chutes, or low waterfalls, and small circular pools, with bubbling jets in each, set in a grass slope with a statue at the bottom as a focal point. At the top of the rill there is a platform and two imposing wooden chairs.

The water emerging from the chutes falls down over copper Vs set in concrete, which are arranged so that the water falling from each chute makes a sound of a different pitch: treble, alto, tenor and bass. This was inspired by the Islamic notion that harmonic chords resonate from falling water. The design came from the formal Mughal gardens in sixteenth- and seventeenth-century India, such as the fine examples of waterfalls in the gardens on Lake Dal in Kashmir. We think that more sensitive ears than ours may be needed to appreciate the sound effect that Jellicoe planned. None the less, this is an extremely pretty rill, and it continues down through the grass into three Islamic-style pools – a square, a hexagon and an octagon – and thence to the statue. Hail to the chutes of Shute House!

The rest of the garden, with its many areas of light and shade playing on the various water features, is hidden from view when looking at this exquisite water rill and waterfalls from the seats at the top but, once the

rill is left behind, the walk along the canal to the magic pool of the spring is a wonderful example of glorious garden-making. There is then a choice of walking down through the woods to another very large reflecting pond and into an enclosed area with some architectural trees, or going over a bridge where one of the many large ponds becomes a small river that runs along the edge of the garden and between the statue and the rill, before arriving at the lawn.

Like all the best gardens, the garden at Shute House has evolved over time. Sir Geoffrey Jellicoe was working on it and changing it up to 1994 (he died in 1996). By then the Trees had sold to the current owners, the Lewises, who have made some changes, originally with Jellicoe's consent. In particular, they have opened up the wide vista over the Dorset landscape. Otherwise, they realise that their responsibility is maintenance, maintenance, maintenance. The apparent simplicity of the water features conceals an elaborate and expensive system of pipes, which have to be kept in very good condition or the springs will emerge in areas where they are not required, and the unique elm wood edgings along the rills and around the pools and borders all need to be looked after.

Water is a fascinating garden element. Sir Geoffrey manipulated and contained it, the Lewises look after it, and we can only admire the interplay of light and shade, smooth and ruffled, silence and sound, reflection and ripples that has been created in this remote corner of south-west England 🌱

THE MAIN SPRING (LEFT) AT SHUTE HOUSE IS THE SOURCE OF THE RIVER NADDER WHICH INSPIRES RELIGIOUS THOUGHTS OF ANCIENT SPIRITS AND PAGAN NYMPHS.

LOWER REACH OF JELLICOE'S RILL (ABOVE) AT SHUTE AND HIS POOLS, BASED ON ISLAMIC GARDEN DESIGN SHAPES.

SUPERB EIGHTEENTH-CENTURY

COURTYARD OF SOMERSET

HOUSE (RIGHT) DESIGNED BY

WILLIAM CHAMBERS, WITH ITS

TWENTY-FIRST-CENTURY GRID

OF FIFTY-FIVE COMPUTER

CONTROLLED WATER JETS.

MAGNIFICENT 'GROVE' OF

WATER JET DISPLAY (OVERLEAF)

IN FULL LIVING COLOURS NOW

GIVING ENDLESS PLEASURE TO

LONDONERS AND VISITORS –

CAN THERE BE CAFÉ LIFE IN

LONDON AFTER GAY PAREE?

Somerset House

THE STRAND, LONDON

Jeremy Dixon and Edward Jones

'Switch off the fountains and you can have a party. That's quite an important aspect that characterises the fountains as being of our time and not of the Edwardian, or some earlier historical time, when you would be totally neutralised: you would have only stood and looked at the basins and their jets.'

Edward Jones on Somerset House

The known history of the Somerset House site starts in the twelfth century, when nobles wishing to influence the Court lived there because of its proximity to Westminster. It had more immediately royal connections when it was the residence of the Lord Protector, the Duke of Somerset, from 1547 until his execution at Tower Hill in 1552. It has been called Somerset House ever since, although it was occupied by various members of the Royal Family until the middle of the eighteenth century.

By 1775 the existing house had become a ruin and George III agreed it could be torn down and the site used for a series of government offices, designed by William Chambers. It also had to accommodate three societies: the Royal Academy of Arts, the Royal Society and the Society of Antiquaries. Chambers solved the differing requirements of these various organisations by making a quadrangle of large town houses, all of which are related architecturally. Internally self-contained, each is six floors high, with four floors rising from the courtyard and two floors going down to river level. At that time the Thames came up to the side of the building, where there was a landing stage, so that it could be approached by the Strand or by the Thames. In the mid-nineteenth century, the construction of the Embankment to strengthen the sides of the Thames meant that the building became separated from the river and Chambers' design for the waterfront is now seen as a rather elaborate sub-structure to the main buildings.

Somerset House remained the head office for the Inland Revenue, and the depository of everybody's wills, until the beginning of the 1990s. Slowly the civil servants were moved out. In 1999, the last of their cars was banned from the parking areas in the Great Courtyard, and many of the buildings now house various extraordinary collections of art, including those of the Courtauld Institute and the Gilbert Collection.

A competition was held to decide what should happen in the courtyard, and inevitably some of the suggestions were quite traditional. These included plans for parterres, groves of trees and other planting areas. The architects who won, Jeremy Dixon and Edward Jones (best known for their wonderful renovations and additions to the Royal Opera House, Covent Garden), saw the space as a *cour d'honneur*. It reminded them of the classical courtyards in France, with their formal water features. They were also aware that we are in the twenty-first century and the technology of water has changed dramatically in the last two centuries – or even the last twenty-five years. They decided to install a dance of water in the centre of the courtyard. This involved removing the existing surface and replacing it with a stone surface which dipped very slightly towards the centre. There had to be sufficient room underneath to install all the technical and electrical equipment necessary for the pumps and computers. Lord Rothschild approached Mrs Lily Safra, who gave a large sum in memory of her husband. Half of this was for the installation of the dance of water and, with amazing practicality, the other half was for its maintenance.

The water feature was completed in 2000 and now plays for twelve hours each day from 10 am to 10 pm. Its 55 jets are arranged as a grid, or quincunx, which is a traditional formal arrangement like the five on a playing card, so the avenues between the jets can be enjoyed from every angle, both straight and on the diagonal. The height of the jets changes from 25cm (10in) to 3m (10ft), in a rhythmic pattern, and are spaced in such a way that it is always possible to walk through them without getting wet, no matter how high they are shooting (unless the wind is blowing furiously in the 'wrong' way).

People are often tentative about walking through the avenues of water until they see other people emerging at the other end quite dry except for the soles of their shoes. Some visitors see it as a magical playground and young children are inclined to remove as many clothes as their parents will allow, giggling and screaming with joy as they dance through the water. At the base of each jet is a four-square fibre optic light fixture which gives an amazing light display at dusk and after dark, enhancing and partnering the water dance. For most of the time the lighting is white, but for ten minutes each hour it changes from white through a variety of colours and patterns, from yellow to pink to red, to dark green and purple. Like the changing patterns of the jets, the changing colours are controlled by a central computer.

Previously, similar displays made of jets of water had been installed in the United States by leading landscape and garden designers, Daniel Kiley and George Hargreaves, but what Jeremy Dixon and Edward Jones have done in the courtyard at Somerset House is unique in Britain. (Interestingly, as Edward Jones remarked to us, these are also the first major public fountains to be installed in London since Sir Edwin Lutyens designed the fountains and pools in Trafalgar Square as his last project, in 1939.)

The water display occupies about a third of the total courtyard space. The rest of the area is available for people to walk through, to sit in, or to have a drink and a meal. People are slowly hearing about the water dance and, though they may go to Somerset House to see the exhibitions or to eat in the restaurant overlooking the Thames, they all stop to look, and are staggered by the water display, by day and night. In the depths of winter, the area becomes an underlit skating rink for a few weeks, using water in a different form, but whatever the season, the display is a magical tribute to twenty-first-century technology

SCULPTOR WILLIAM PYE'S
SUPERB CONTEMPORARY
BRONZE ANTONY CONE (RIGHT)
SET IN TRADITIONAL GARDENS
OF COUNTRY HOUSE, ANTONY,
SEAT OF THE POLE CAREW
FAMILY.

THE IMPOSING VENERABLE
YEW TOPIARY CONE (OPPOSITE)
WAS PYE'S INSPIRATION FOR HIS
WATER SCULPTURE, ANTONY
CONE.

ANTONY

TORPOINT, CORNWALL

William Pye

'It is certainly true the great water features of the eighteenth and nineteenth centuries, or even earlier in Italy, were demonstrations of power. I'm not interested in that element, but I am preoccupied with controlling water, but in a quiet way. I am more interested in how water flows naturally through a spout than how it disgorges out of a high-pressure jet. It is something to do with the simplicity of gravity.'

William Pye on Antony

The Carew Poles have lived at Antony in Cornwall for more than six centuries and, even though the house and the surrounding 12 hectares (29 acres) now belong to the National Trust, the family continues to live there. Sir Richard Carew Pole moved into the house in 1983. In 2001 he was elected Chairman of the Royal Horticultural Society.

The house has grown and changed during their ownership, its classical Georgian façade hiding many features that are a reminder of its medieval origins. The garden, too, has seen many changes over the centuries. The formal parterres to the north of the house, planted by Sir William Carew in the early eighteenth century, were swept away in the 1790s and replaced by Humphry Repton with more open, naturalistic, grassy vistas around the house. In the nineteenth century Sir William Henry Pole Carew returned formality to the garden and planted the great yew walk to the west of the house, and Sir Reginald added very elaborate flower gardens where Sir William Carew's parterres had originally been.

Inevitably, because of the dramatic reduction in the number of people looking after the garden, those parterres have gone and the garden is much simplified. But the great yew walk is still there, with an enormous Mandalay bell as a focal point at one end. To one side is a very large conical yew topiary with a shady arbour

within its confines that was used by Lady Beatrice Pole Carew to watch tennis at the end of the nineteenth century. A path in front of the Mandalay bell leads past two nineteenth-century painted lead figures of a shepherd and shepherdess, given to Sir John Pole Carew by his mother-in-law in 1950. She also constructed a sheltered summer garden, seen through an archway in a yew hedge that encloses another area of the garden.

One thing the gardens lacked was a water feature. In 1995, having seen a water sculpture by William Pye at the Royal Academy of Arts in London, Sir Richard Carew Pole sent him a postcard, asking him to come and look at the gardens. He duly did so, and it was suggested that he make a water feature in the West Lawn. This is quite close to the house, in a direct line of sight to the giant yew cone, whose top can be seen rising above the yew hedge. This shape inspired William Pye to suggest that his sculpture should take the form of a bronze cone, 3m (10ft) high, covered with a sheen of water.

The effect of the water depends entirely upon the light or shade on any given day: sometimes it will glisten and sometimes it will be a very faint sheen. The bronze is weathering beautifully under the water sheen, and the exquisite sound of water gently falling into the reservoir pool around the cone can be heard by anyone standing very close to the sculpture.

The placing of the Antony Cone is equally subtle. William Pye drew two lines, one from the west door of the house and another from the top of the stairs. From either of these two viewing points, the angle of the cone is such that the eye is taken to it and then upwards to the sky. This is exactly the game that Holbein used in his famous picture, *The Ambassadors*, now at the National Gallery, where a shape at the base of the picture suddenly becomes a skull when viewed from a different angle. There is very strong geometry about the way the paving to the sculpture has been designed so that both eye and feet are led to the point from which William Pye wishes the sculpture to be viewed. In this way, the sculptor has tried to impose an anamorphic point of view on the cone.

William Pye says that it is not so much a contemporary design as a sculpture inspired by the setting in which it is placed. It is only contemporary because of the materials he has used. The most interesting thing is that the National Trust, the owners of Antony and its garden, have allowed such a water feature to be placed within a very traditional landscape. As an organisation they are much concerned with their responsibility to the gardens which they hold in trust. There are those who think that all their gardens should be frozen in time and maintained at whatever particular year the National Trust deems the perfect year, decade or century for that landscape. There is also a very strong voice that says quite correctly that every garden and every landscape changes every year and that most great gardens are great because their owners have been innovative.

THE EFFECT OF THE WATER DEPENDS ENTIRELY UPON THE LIGHT OR SHADE ON ANY GIVEN DAY: SOMETIMES IT WILL GLISTEN AND SOMETIMES IT WILL BE A VERY FAINT SHEEN.

Many of the National Trust's gardens are high maintenance, which means the costs grow exponentially and may soon be beyond their budget. The garden at Antony has evolved over a very long period and is much simpler than it has been for many generations, but it now has a water feature which is essential for every garden. The fact that the water feature depends for its effect on current technology makes it an entirely suitable and relevant feature in such a historic garden

THE ELEGANT DESIGN
MARRIAGE OF SIMPLICITY
(OPPOSITE) ACROSS THE
CENTURIES: CLIPPED YEWS OF
THE EIGHTEENTH AND THE
BRONZE ANTONY CONE OF OUR
TIME, THE TWENTY-FIRST.

ANTHONY ARCHER-WILLS'
NATURALISTIC LAKE (RIGHT) IS
INCLUSIVE GARDEN DESIGN FOR
THE HOUSE, WITH THE 'CLIFF-
HANGING' COMPLETELY
CANTILEVERED WOODEN
TERRACE IN THE FOREGROUND.

WHAT ENDLESS PLEASURE

THE OWNERS HAVE IN ALL
SEASONS (OPPOSITE) WITH THIS
LAKE PROSPECT FROM THEIR
CONSERVATORY IN WEST
SUSSEX.

THE HAPPY RELATIONSHIP

OF THE LAKE, JUST TWO YEARS
OLD, AND THE HOUSE
(OVERLEAF) IS PARTIALLY
ATTRIBUTED TO THE
NATURALISTIC FORM OF THIS
EXCELLENT LARGE WATER
FEATURE.

Naturalistic Lake

STORRINGTON, WEST SUSSEX

Anthony Archer-Wills

Anthony Archer-Wills fell in love with pools as a very small boy at boarding school. On Sundays the pupils were allowed to wander in the woods around the school. There he found springs and ponds which he dammed into pools, and became obsessed with water and the way it looks, what happens in it, how it changes temperature and colour, as well as with the birds and insects that are attracted to it. At home, there was a lake near his parents' farm which was very deep and clear. He was fascinated by looking through the water and seeing its shimmering, glittering bed.

He started his own business in 1964 and one of his very first jobs was for the Duke of Bedford at Woburn Abbey. Since then he has become recognised as the person who understands water in the landscape better than anybody else in Great Britain. We first met him when we were both installing major lakes for a rock star. On that estate, which was on clay, the lakes were

dug out and then puddled, or compacted to increase water retention. This is the traditional way of making lakes in the landscape where the soil and water supply are suitable, and the clay has to be at least 30cm (12in) deep throughout. The junction between water and earth is the most critical point of any lake or pond, whether it is puddled or lined with concrete or butyl. (Butyl linings are fine for large ponds, but Anthony Archer-Wills does not recommend them for lakes as they only last for about fifteen years.)

The lake at Storrington was made at the bottom of the garden, on a 0.8 hectare (2 acre) site that had previously been a field. Anthony Archer-Wills' concept was to make the lake as large as possible, but to fool the eye when the lake is first seen from the conservatory that looks out across the landscape. From there, the lake appears to narrow on the far right-hand side, and its sides are hidden. The whole of the lake can only be seen from the

garden itself. It then becomes apparent that the soil excavated from the lake has been used to make a series of natural-looking earth forms around three sides of the lake, to act as a berm, or containing bank. In the middle of the lake are two small islands, where birds can nest safely.

THE LAKE WAS FINISHED IN 1999 AND NOW SITS VERY HAPPILY IN THE LANDSCAPE.

The garden is on clay, so the lake was puddled and its shape is naturalistic, giving the impression of an expanse of water that has been there for a long time. The source of the lake is a spring near its furthest tip, which was tested by Anthony Archer-Wills to ensure that its flow was strong enough to keep the lake full and refreshed at all times of the year. This is vital, because the owners wanted to avoid algae forming in their lake.

Since water is flowing through the lake constantly, and the lake is at least 2m (6ft) deep, and in some areas goes down to 8m (26ft), it is extremely unlikely that algae will be a problem.

Paths have been mown through the grass on the earth forms, making a circuit round the lake and encouraging exploration from every angle. Halfway up on the left-hand side is a summerhouse with a wooden pier or terrace that is splendidly cantilevered over the water. Trees have been planted on the grass-covered earth banks, and plants that love being near or in water are thriving around the edges. The lake was finished in 1999 and now sits very happily in the landscape. Many of the trees, particularly the fast-growing willows, look as if they have been there for years. One of the owners is an obsessed gardener and, with the help of her handyman, makes sure that the lake is beautifully maintained, with the grass berms mown and the shrubs kept pruned and neat ❦

THE SIMPLE BACKLIT

LAMINATED GLASS SCREEN

(RIGHT) IS AN EXCELLENT FOIL

AND CONTRAST TO DICKSONIA

OR TASMANIAN TREE FERN.

THINNEST AND LIGHTEST-

WEIGHT ALUMINIUM CYLINDERS

FILLED WITH PLANTS (OPPOSITE)

DO REALLY FLOAT IN A MOST

CHARMING WAY; AN IDEA PAUL

COOPER ADAPTED FROM A

MIDDLE EASTERN PROJECT.

Floating Gardens

EPPING, ESSEX

Paul Cooper

Some years ago Paul Cooper entered a competition to design a garden for a palace in Dubai. Since Dubai is in a desert, he decided there had to be water. He conceived the brilliant idea that the plants would be floating in containers in the water feature, rather than being stationary around the water, as is more usual. The prince would have had the Floating Gardens of Dubai. Sadly, Paul Cooper was not awarded the project, but a few years later he used the same idea in another of his controversial gardens at the Chelsea Flower Show in 1999.

The owners saw the floating gardens and asked him to install that element in their garden. They have lived in their house for almost thirty years and the garden is the width of the house, which is about 12m (40ft), and about 6m (20ft) in depth. There is a tall wall along the back, beyond which is a very tall leylandii hedge, giving privacy from the hotel which would otherwise overlook the garden. One of the owners has always been a very keen gardener so there was a border around the perimeters and a grass area in the middle, where the children played. The children have gone and Paul Cooper decided the garden needed refocusing.

THE LIGHTING IN THIS GARDEN REFLECTS HIS SHORT INVOLVEMENT WITH THEATRICAL DESIGN.

He did not want the viewer to be aware of the whole garden at once, so he made two focal points, effectively in each corner of the garden. The lawn was taken out, hard surface materials such as decking and gravel went down, and in one corner a polygonal pond was installed in which five floating containers were placed. These are made of polystyrene with a very light stainless-steel surround, and have a hole in the bottom so the plants can

absorb water from the pond, and lose excess water when it rains. Nobody knew quite which plants would be suitable for this unusual environment, and changes are made all the time. The day we were there, the owners were talking about changing the plants for the winter to heathers and ericas. At the back, a rectangular feature has just been installed which makes a decorative feature of the water source in the pool. It includes a screen which masks a back-projected video, whose images change at the owners' whim. The screen is framed by tubular lights which create moving light as they bounce off each other.

In the other corner there are three trellis panels, placed one behind the other and decreasing in size to give an optical illusion of depth. At the back of the panels is another laminated glass screen with a tree fern in front. This is backlit at night, adding a different but effective lighting element in that part of the garden. Paul Cooper is certain that every garden should be lit, so

that it can be enjoyed by its owners at all times of the year. The lighting in this garden reflects his short involvement with theatrical design. As he says, 'Clients in the main are out of the house and garden all day. Most people only see their gardens at dusk, or in the evening, and summer doesn't last that long, so on winter evenings [six long British months, in our opinion] when you come home the garden is absolutely black and dark. Therefore, it seems essential to try and make the garden work with lighting all year round.'

These then are the Floating Gardens of Dubai in a comparatively small British garden. When Paul Cooper was reminiscing about his original inspiration from the Middle East, the land of the Bible, he remembered thinking of coracles drifting across a bare surface of water, so perhaps he was imagining, slightly fantastically, the basket in which Moses was found amongst the bulrushes

sculpture

A roaring motorcar . . . is more beautiful than the Nike of Samothrace.

Filippo Marinetti (1909)

BARBARA HEPWORTH PLACED
HER GREAT SCULPTURES
(PREVIOUS PAGE) JUST OUTSIDE
HER ST IVES STUDIO IN THE
GARDEN SHE DESIGNED WITH A
FRIEND, COMPOSER PRIAULX
RAINIER.

COLOURED CONCRETE IN THE
GARDEN IS ONE OF MANY
CRAFT SPECIALITIES (RIGHT) OF
CAROLE VINCENT, ALSO LIVING
IN CORNWALL, AND MAKES
THESE UNIQUE AND STRONGLY
COLOURED STRIATED CONCRETE
SCULPTURES.

Every garden needs one or two elements that do not change throughout the year, and these are likely to be sculptural. They may be made of evergreen material (usually box, yew or ivy), in the form of topiary. Or they may be constructed of solid materials such as stone, bronze, lead or wood, and are sculptures. Such elements ornament the garden at any time of the year, but may also be positioned as eye-catchers. These act as focal points for the eye or draw a visitor to another viewing point. They may also lead to an area whose existence had not been suspected, so providing the best part of garden exploration – a surprise!

Statues have been used in these ways since classical times, and the trend was revived by the Medicis in Florence at the end of the fifteenth century, when gardens became more formal. Statuary was designed specifically for use in the landscape, and Roman sculpture was excavated and reinstated in the gardens of the new princes of power, both in the many small principalities and in the states controlled by popes and their 'nephews'. At Hadrian's villa, outside Rome, some of the pillars and statues originally ordered by Hadrian were found and replaced in the positions the emperor would have known.

In the seventeenth and eighteenth centuries there

was a mania for enhancing grand landscapes with statues. Italian and Dutch gardens, in particular, had strong, architectural layouts (put into the mind's eye the formality of the gardens at Villa Lante or Het Loo). Long vistas or *allées* led from the main façades of the house. Sometimes these were made up of a series of rooms, created by tall hedges or walls, so that the eye looks through one room to another and is intrigued by a focal point, perhaps a statue or an obelisk, in the distance. This was very good business for sculptors. It also meant that the idea of using objects in the landscape permeated the minds of garden makers. (Nowadays, statues in very small gardens may have become gnomes or images of dogs, rabbits, or birds, but the idea is the same, whatever its level of sophistication.)

Living garden statuary in the form of topiary also has a long history (indeed, the Latin name for gardener was *topiarius*). The fact that it is made of plant material which grows, changes and eventually dies means that we only know how topiary was used in the past from etchings and prints that were made at the time. However, topiary is not a very difficult art to master: it only requires the determination to create a certain image and the guts to clip and trim vigorously every year. A suitable plant can be simply clipped to form a ball, a cone or an obelisk. Complicated shapes are easily achieved by forming them round a chicken-wire structure of the desired image; box or ivy is grown into the frame and clipped to fit. Yew can also be grown into wire frames (we have seen a line of topiary hounds chase a topiary fox – now, alas, so politically incorrect!).

Topiary skills can be deployed in other areas of the garden. Hedges have long been used to divide one part of the garden from another, and may be pruned so they have a battlemented topping. Even the despised leylandii becomes an elegant screen when it is clipped twice a year, and is very effective if you wish to hide your garden frolics from the neighbours.

Contemporary sculpture sits well in a garden, as the bronze creations of Dame Barbara Hepworth demonstrate. Her garden in now part of Tate St Ives in Cornwall. The Carole Vincent garden in Cornwall is inspired by her most imaginative use of coloured concrete, both for the hard landscape ground plane of the garden, but also for geometric sculptures used as focal points within it. The found objects, or *objets trouvés*, which have caught the imagination of Ivan Hicks (department store dress dummies painted all over with a pattern of clouds and sky influenced by Magritte, the great Belgian surrealist) are a splendidly witty form of contemporary garden sculpture.

Gardens have always changed and in Great Britain people are increasingly designing and installing gardens that celebrate the twenty-first century. These may include site-specific or site-generated sculptures, which we consider the most exciting form of contemporary sculpture (allied to an equally important theory of garden and landscape design). Such sculptures emerge when a sculptor is inspired by a particular site and creates a sculpture specific to that site and no other. The glades of a wood in Kent (very close to that epitome of the English garden, with its geometric plan and tumbling plantings, Sissinghurst) have become the site of a number of these sculptures. They can be made of myriad materials, including rusty metal, twigs or interlocking pieces of wood, piles of shingle or mounds of stone. In this landscape, called the Gardens of Gaia, you never know what you may find, but visiting such a place could inspire everybody to place the unexpected permanent element in their own back garden

THREE WEST GREEN

GARDENERS (RIGHT): LIVING
AND BREATHING ARE DOMINIC
RENDELL WITH WATERING CAN
AND DAVID CHASE WITH SPADE,
AND IN STONE IS THOMAS
MANN, A GARDENER THERE FOR
FORTY YEARS.

AN ITALIAN BAROQUE-STYLE
NYMPHAEUM (OPPOSITE) IS
EXTREMELY RARE IN GREAT
BRITIAN. THIS BEAUTIFUL
EXAMPLE DRAWN BY QUINLAN
TERRY HAS ENCHANTING RILL
AND WATER STEPS AS ITS
OPENING BEATS.

West Green House

HARTLEY WINTNEY, HAMPSHIRE

Marylyn Abbott

est Green House was built at the very beginning of the eighteenth century by General Henry Hawley and its structure has remained essentially unchanged since then. One garden façade of the house has five niches in which there have always been classical busts of Roman dignitaries, but almost nothing remains of Hawley's garden apart from a moon gate in an original brick wall. (This now frames a view of the late-twentieth-century nymphaeum by the brilliant retro-Palladian architect, Quinlan Terry.)

Around 1900, the Playfair family employed the architect Robert Weir Schultz to remodel the north front of the house and design new gardens. Five years later, Evelyn, Duchess of Wellington, bought the house and, with her friend Yvonne Fitzroy, redesigned the gardens. The result was so inspiring that the gardens were featured in a *Country Life* article in the 1930s. They changed little over the next few decades.

Having been left to the National Trust in 1957, the House became the property of the Trust after Miss Fitzroy's death in 1971. The first tenant was Lord McAlpine, who transformed the gardens into a romantic, timeless Elysium. With the help of Quinlan Terry, the landscape was reorganised so that there were enclosed areas and open vistas, with long walks always culminating in eye-catchers. Thus an obelisk to a Labour Chancellor stands at the end of an avenue of trees leading from the original entrance to the house. A nymphaeum (originally a shrine or grotto dedicated to the nymphs, with fountains and pools, which later evolved into an architectural wall form) is seen through the moon gate, together with its rills and ponds. Beside a new lake stands another obelisk, against which leans a statue of Lord McAlpine's favourite gardener, Mr Mann, who worked in the garden for forty years.

McAlpine had wanted to create a landscape that was

somewhere between pleasing decay and neglect, and neglected the garden certainly became because the house was rocked by an IRA bomb five months after he left in 1990. Three years later, Marylyn Abbott, an Australian, fell in love with the house and its surrounding gardens. Marylyn Abbott is a very knowledgeable gardener, having a house and garden of almost similar size in Kennerton Green, near Mittagong in New South

> WHATEVER THE SIZE OF YOUR GARDEN, 'BY CLIPPING YOUR GREEN MATERIAL TO WHATEVER SHAPE OR SIZE PLEASES YOU, YOU CAN HAVE YOUR OWN GREEN SCULPTURE'.

Wales, which has been open to the public for many years. She has her own views about how gardens and landscapes should look and, although she was aware that an amazing amount of money and patience would

be needed to restore the gardens and make them match her vision, she took on a ninety-nine-year lease.

Some things had to change. The 1930s swimming pool was filled in, and has now become a topiary garden in which all the figures are modelled on characters Alice met in Wonderland: the Rabbit, the Red Queen, the Mad Hatter, and the Dormouse, for example. This garden was planted in 1997 and the topiary figures, all on wire frames and realised in box, have become almost perfect representations of their fantasy characters. In another part of the garden, unusual rings of neatly clipped box grow round the base of some apple trees. As Marylyn Abbott says, whatever the size of your garden, 'by clipping your green material to whatever shape or size pleases you, you can have your own green sculpture'.

Marylyn Abbott has clear ideas about the plants that she wishes to grow. She also recognises the importance of maintenance and understands how much can be

SUPERB AND UNUSUAL
BOXWOOD HEDGES (ABOVE)
SCULPTURALLY EMBRACE APPLE
TREES AT THE SIDE ENTRANCE
TO WEST GREEN HOUSE.

BIRD'S-EYE-VIEW PAINTING
(LEFT) COMMISSIONED BY
MARYLYN ABBOTT, CHATELAINE
OF WEST GREEN HOUSE, WHO
HAS SENSITIVELY RESTORED AND
CONTINUES TO IMPROVE
BEAUTIFULLY THESE GARDENS.

THE IMMACULATELY KEMPT
FORMAL POTAGER (OPPOSITE)
WITH CHINOISERIE-STYLE FRUIT
CAGE AND MARYLYN ABBOTT'S
AMUSING ADDITION OF A FAT
WATTLE BOAT AND TEPEE.

properly looked after by three gardeners. In the main enclosed garden, there are mixed borders and flower beds all around the walls. The colours change seasonally through the year, as do some of the plants. Beyond the borders are two very large black Chinoiserie circular fruit cages, originally erected in the garden's former recreation, enclosing raspberries, gooseberries and currants, because the birds love them so much that they need to be protected. The vegetables in the formal beds around these cages change dramatically every year. When we saw them, painted tripods of blue, red and purple had been placed amongst them to act as supports where needed and to provide visual contrast. By them is a large fat wattle barque which is planted with herbs and other perennials.

The water around the nymphaeum has been changed and reorganised. It now flows through a single central rill before dividing into two narrow stone rills along the sides of the paving, needing less maintenance than the irregular stones which had been casually strewn there by the previous leaseholder. The lakes have been cleared so that they again reflect the obelisk and the gardener statue, and a gazebo has been erected on an island in one of them.

The gardens at West Green are all about change. Marylyn Abbott knows that she is a temporary custodian, but she loves the house and garden and her fine eye and aesthetic skills show in the sensitive improvements she has made. By realising her own vision of horticultural beauty, she has imprinted her personality and dreams upon this landscape. Future tenants may have different views and, though it is likely that the stone buildings and sculptures will survive, perhaps the Mad Hatter and the Dormouse will be replaced by other topiary sculptures in the years to come

THIS BAROQUE FOCAL POINT
(RIGHT) SEEMS TO BE MADE OF
ASHLAR STONE DESIGNED BY
BORROMINI OR HAWKSMOOR.
NO, IT'S MADE OF PACKING
CASES CLEVERLY CRAFTED BY
GEORGE CARTER, TO *TROMPE
LES YEUX* HERE.

HORNBEAM HEDGE ALLÉE
(OPPOSITE) WITH CHARMING
RECYCLED GARDEN HANDTOOL
GATE ECHOES SEVENTEENTH-
CENTURY FRENCH DESIGN.
FINIAL ON THE PYRAMID IS
A GILDED BALLCOCK; CARTER
IS BOTH PRACTICAL AND
HUMOROUS.

Silverstone Farm

NORFOLK

George Carter

'If I had to declare a purpose in creating this garden, beyond that of having fun, I would admit to attempting to reinvent a sort of neo-Palladian style of gardening suitable for now, and viewed, as it were, in the light of Modernism. So although references to Classicism and the Antique abound, the detail is very pared down and simplified and often carried out using modern or unexpected materials . . . grandeur of effect without appearing pretentious.'

George Carter on Silverstone Farm

George Carter has lived in Norfolk for twenty-five years but only found Silverstone Farm about ten years ago. He was looking for a small but perfectly proportioned house, preferably with a few outbuildings, and a garden that extended in all directions from the house. Silverstone Farm almost exactly matched his requirements except that the main front of

the house is unbalanced because of the interior arrangement of the staircase: a green vertical of wisteria has been placed next to the front door, so the eye is fooled into believing the façade is Palladian in its inspiration.

The first thing George Carter did was to extend two screen or wing walls on either side of the house going up to first-floor level and meeting the walls which had always enclosed the front garden. These extensions were inspired by Humphry Repton, the great early nineteenth-century landscape gardener, who said that such screening walls increase the apparent size of a house, making it look bigger or grander than it actually is.

Immediately outside the front door there are two parterres, planted with santolina and edged in box, like many of the small beds. By the house are some wonderful clipped pyramids of hawthorn, a very quick- and dense-growing shrub which is rarely used in topiary. The garden is also enclosed on two sides with tall

hawthorn hedges, but most of the hedging is hornbeam, which is tolerant of a wide range of climatic conditions and will put up with drought or wet. It also has the advantage of growing quite quickly and maintains all its leaves from ground level upwards, providing a well-furnished bottom. Hornbeam hedges were used a great deal in the seventeenth century to separate the formal areas of the garden from the *bosquets*.

George Carter really only likes green-on-green, the contrast of one green leaf against another, and allows only one type of white climbing rose in his garden: Rambling Rector. He uses a fairly small palette of plant material. Plants he favours for making topiary shapes include Portuguese laurel and phillyrea, a shrub to which John Evelyn was constantly referring in his famous diaries when writing about the gardens that he visited all round Europe. This is now more difficult to find, but George Carter has a very dark green variety with an olive-shaped leaf. He also has some topiary made from holm oak and sometimes uses a small-leafed privet grafted on to large-leafed privet.

Italian and Dutch gardens, particularly those of the seventeenth century with their vistas and *allées* have been an important influence on George Carter, as has William Kent (1685–1748), who was a great Italophile. He used his artistic talents to design theatre sets, furniture, a whole house or merely its interiors and, of course, the garden or landscape surrounding it: Kent designs are extant for the interiors at Chiswick and Wilton Houses, and the landscape at Rousham House.

From the front of the house, a small gate leads into a grass area known as the tennis lawn. At the end is a William Kent-inspired obelisk, which looks as though it is stone, but is actually made of recycled packing cases that have lasted for twenty years. It is set against a background of trees that camouflage the view of the fields beyond. Behind the house, a gate made of garden implements leads to the Green Theatre. This is inspired by the *teatro di verdura* at the Villa Reale di Marlia, outside Lucca in Italy, which is the climax of a very formal area in the grounds of a grand house. There, the theatre is discovered by the sound of a very tall jet of water, which has a circle of yew round it. Behind this is the theatre stage, a large semicircle with terracotta statues of *commedia dell'arte* figures in arched recesses behind the stage. Carter has simplified the original design by placing urns in his five arches, pruned out of Lawson's cypress, with five clipped box balls immediately in front on the grass, representing the fantasy stage lighting.

A long grass sward leads from the side of the house through an enclosed area, via an avenue of pleached lime, to a wall fountain on one of the façades of the barn. A shorter grass sward leads to the herb garden, where there is a garden seat in the style of Kent (a copy of the hall seats found in Italian villas or loggias). Beyond the herb garden is an old toolshed which has had a slightly rusticated, baroque

façade added to it. It terminates one of the vistas and has been renamed the Temple of Convenience, an outdoor WC made classic and formal with grandiose columns, reminding people how far they would have had to walk in an eighteenth-century garden when nature 'called'.

Some years ago, George Carter built a small *trompe l'oeil* garden at the Chelsea Flower Show. He achieved an amazing effect of formality in an area only 3m (10ft) wide and 6m (20ft) long by building a series of trellis arches, diminishing in size from front to back, and ending with a doorway which appeared to be full size but was actually in miniature. He has discovered that many of the seventeenth- and eighteenth-century eye-catchers were made of wood, because it was an inexpensive way of creating an image for a vista if an owner could not afford longer-lasting materials. Apparently, there were more carpenters than gardeners at Versailles, when Louis XIV was 'fooling the eye'.

The spaces George Carter creates are magical, and many of his ideas could easily be adapted to gardens of any size. Because his gardens are created with evergreen plant material that only needs trimming once or twice a year, the maintenance level is fairly low. His client list is very impressive, so there are clearly a lot of people who love the idea of formality in the landscape and feel at ease in the regulated seclusion of his green-on-green world

EXEDRA OR SEMICIRCULAR

HORNBEAM HEDGE (LEFT) MAKES A THEATRE SCENE WITH URN DECORATIONS AND BOXWOOD FOOTLIGHTS; IT COULD BE A PICTURE IN A GRAND SIXTEENTH- OR SEVENTEENTH-CENTURY FORMAL ITALIAN OR FRENCH GARDEN.

CARTER'S DESIGN AESTHETIC

IS MAINLY GREEN AND FORMAL. HE ALLOWS ONE WHITE CLIMBING ROSE, RAMBLING RECTOR (ABOVE). THE PRETTY LEAD FROSTWORK FOUNTAIN'S FINIAL IS, YES, ANOTHER GILDED BALLCOCK.

EXTREMELY RARE GRAECO-ROMAN PORPHYRY BOWL (RIGHT) UNDER ITS VERY OWN CANOPY PLACED TO BE THE FOCAL POINT AT THE CROSSING OF FORMAL HEDGE AND TREE ALLÉES. THE DARK RED STONE IS HARMONIOUS WITH THE COPPER BEECH HEDGE.

THE RE-PLANTING OF NEW YOUNG SPRUCE TREES, 1988 (OPPOSITE) MAKES THE EMPEROR'S WALK AND BACKS BUSTS OF THE ROMAN CAESARS. IN 2001, THE STATUES ARE PARTIALLY HIDDEN BY THE TREES' VIGOROUS GROWTH.

A MOST SPLENDID STATUE OF THE GODDESS OF PAINTING, ATHENA (OVERLEAF), THOUGHT TO HAVE COME FROM THE EIGHTEENTH-CENTURY GARDEN WITH THE GREATEST COLLECTION OF CLASSICAL GARDEN BUILDINGS, STOWE.

Anglesey Abbey

LODE, CAMBRIDGESHIRE

Anglesey Abbey dates back to medieval times and, though the house has changed considerably over many centuries, it still appears to be a sixteenth-century building. The first Lord Fairhaven, Huttleston Broughton, aggrandised it in the 1930s because he wanted sufficient space to accommodate his guests and the trappings of his lifestyle, including a library and the many paintings and objects he continued to acquire throughout his life.

His family background was one of much American money combined with British taste, and his view of his gardens was that of the traditional English gentleman. He wished to show the world how rich he was but was equally concerned that his house should be surrounded by gardens and views of beauty. This was quite difficult in the Fen country, north of Cambridge, because the land is flat and the winds blow from the east with great ferocity at many times of year. Being a sensible man, the first thing

he did was to create a shelter belt of trees around the entire 40 hectares (100 acres) of his garden. He then proceeded to define and embellish the landscape with statuary.

At Anglesey Abbey there are avenues of great formality, interspersed with wooded areas. One of the formal walks from the house leads to a water feature from which can be seen a large Italian baroque-inspired canopy, an outdoor *baldacchino*, protecting a wonderful and precious late-Roman artefact, the Porphyry Bowl. Walking closer to the canopy, the visitor becomes aware that there is a large circular area, almost surrounded by a tall copper beech hedge, on the far side. Within the beech circle are statues of four Greek goddesses, representing the arts. They are superb examples of eighteenth-century statuary and are thought to have come from a truly great garden of that period, Stowe in Buckinghamshire.

An immense avenue of clipped yew now comes into

view, stretching to right and left of the Porphyry Bowl. This is the Emperors' Walk, which was one of the first features to be planted and is 400m (¼ mile) long. Eighteenth-century allegorical statues act as focal points at either end. Along one side of the Emperors' Walk, just proud of the spruce trees, are busts of the twelve Roman emperors, amongst them Tiberius, Claudius, Nero, Augustus and Hadrian. These embellish the long vista wonderfully.

Such statues were first used to ornament gardens and landscapes in classical times and then again from the late fifteenth century onwards. Over the centuries, many of them have been removed or lost, sold or destroyed, as well as being endlessly copied and reproduced in the eighteenth century (as they are now). It is remarkable that Lord Fairhaven was able to find such a fine collection of statuary, of the kind that would have been selected by an eighteenth-century aristocrat who wished to re-create the gardens he had visited in France and Italy while on a Grand Tour. It is equally remarkable that the collection has remained where he decreed it would be placed. Of his 40 hectares (100 acres) of landscape, 14 hectares (35 acres) are mown lawn, which needed a large gardening staff while he lived there. Lord Fairhaven was a tidy man, and he would have been pleased that the acres of lawn continue to be scrupulously maintained, so these statues are still in a beautifully manicured sylvan setting.

As Sir Arthur Bryant wrote in 1964: 'Our age is not without rich men, yet . . . Huttleston Fairhaven must be almost unique in having created in the middle of the twentieth century a garden which can compare with the great masterpieces of the Georgian era. With patience, single-minded devotion and flawless taste, in an age of war and revolution, he has endowed the England of tomorrow with a garden worthy of her past.'

TWO FORMS (DIVIDED CIRCLE), 1970 (RIGHT) IN THE BARBARA HEPWORTH MUSEUM, AN ADJUNCT OF THE TATE ST IVES, CORNWALL.

DOWN VIEW OF GARDEN (OPPOSITE) AT HEPWORTH MUSEUM, INCLUDING TWO FORMS AND RIVER FORM, 1965, SHOT FROM THE FIRST FLOOR SHOWING THE GARDEN AND STUDIO IN CONTEXT OF THE TOWN.

Trewyn Studio

ST IVES, CORNWALL

Dame Barbara Hepworth and Priaulx Rainier

Barbara Hepworth was born in Yorkshire in 1903, but she moved to St Ives in Cornwall in 1939 with her husband, the painter Ben Nicholson, and their three children, and lived there for the rest of her life. As a child she loved dancing, music, drawing and painting (including the gorgeous smell of paint!). She absorbed the contours of her native Yorkshire when travelling in her father's car, later observing that 'the hills were sculptures and the roads defined form'. In Cornwall she found 'a background which links with Yorkshire in the natural shape of stone structures and fertility, and it links with Italy because of the light and colour.'

The first years in Cornwall were difficult: the family had little money, the children were still young, and living anywhere during the war was not easy. She passed the immensely high wall surrounding Trewyn Studio many times before she finally entered the front door leading from the street and discovered what became her secret grove. Here, she could be in the middle of town yet entirely hidden from the noise and bustle of St Ives, aware that the beach, the shore, the sea and the curving rocks of Cornwall were easily accessible and could be visited as she wished. The house was just big enough to house her family, who were soon to go their separate ways. There was space in the garden for her workshop, where she could carve out of doors all year round. Most importantly, she had a dear friend called Priaulx Rainier, an accomplished composer but an even more obsessed gardener, who was happy to help with the design of the garden.

The house is built on the side of a hill, with the garden rising behind it, so they decided to make a series of levels in the slope. From a first-floor landing there is access to a comparatively flat area which contains an amazing bronze construction called *Four-square Walk*

THE MAGNIFICENT TOTEMIC
CONVERSATION WITH MAGIC
STONES, 1973 (LEFT) WAS THE
SCULPTOR'S LAST IMPORTANT
BRONZE.
DANCING WATER
REFLECTIONS ENHANCE
SUPERBLY THE HEPWORTH
SCULPTURE (OPPOSITE)
FROM 1965, RIVER FORM.

Through, made in 1966; beyond that is *Two forms (divided circle)* (1969), also made of bronze. These were both designed for their specific locations so that the garden and the plants could be viewed through them at different angles. They are amazingly tactile – *Two forms (divided circle)* particularly so – because the texture and feel of a sculpture were almost as important to Dame Barbara as its form and shape. She wanted everybody to explore her sculptures as they wished, and would have been horrified by so many museums' current admonition to visitors: 'Do not touch'. Barbara Hepworth was not particularly interested in colour though she did make a few colour pieces. Most of her sculptures are either metal or stone. They might have dull or shiny surfaces but she rarely tampered with the colour of her materials.

Within the plan of the garden she insisted on enclosed planting areas, surrounding the inner with the outer world, as if protecting the child in the womb. She planted *Magnolia grandiflora*, a few flowering cherries and a gingko, because it was one of the oldest trees in existence. Elsewhere there were palms, yuccas, phormiums, cordylines and agapanthus and a wide range of other shrubs, flowering plants, exotics, herbs, trees and bamboos. In the first garden, Rainier had persuaded her

> SHE WANTED EVERYBODY TO EXPLORE HER SCULPTURES AS THEY WISHED, AND WOULD HAVE BEEN HORRIFIED BY SO MANY MUSEUMS' CURRENT ADMONITION TO VISITORS: 'DO NOT TOUCH'.

she should have roses and there were always roses close to the house. She was interested in the shapes of leaves but not in flowers and though she would graciously accept bouquets, they would quietly be dumped as soon as possible.

An early sculpture called *Coré* (1955–6) sits happily in the herbaceous and shrub border, disguising the path to a higher level where there is a collection of truly splendid bronze shapes called *Conversation with Magic Stones* (1973), set against a background of very dark green bamboos which move in the wind. Each sculpture was placed with the intuitive eye of a great artist, and throughout her lifetime Dame Barbara Hepworth used the garden as her gallery, so that people could come and see her latest works in an environment in which she considered them suitably effective. Many sculptures came and went but, by the time she died in a fire in 1975, she had decided that all the sculptures in place in the garden at her death should remain there in perpetuity. And so they have, because the Barbara Hepworth Museum and Sculpture Garden is now part of the Tate St Ives gallery.

Dame Barbara Hepworth and Henry Moore are the only sculptors in Great Britain to have a sculpture park or garden dedicated solely to their work (Henry Moore is memorialised in sculpture parks in Hertfordshire and Yorkshire). Interestingly, both were born in Yorkshire and knew each other quite well when they were growing up, but their lives diverged and now their memorial gardens at either end of England could hardly be further apart.

Almost a quarter of a century after her death, her garden remains an inspiring, stylish and sensual interaction between the sculptures and the garden which she created. It has been maintained so as to embrace and enhance the sculptures it contains, as it did during this great sculptor's lifetime. The thousands of visitors who come to the garden every year continue to see Barbara Hepworth's own particular vision of an artist's paradise

BEAUTIFULLY COLOURED

SHARP CONCRETE CONES (RIGHT)

CREATED BY CAROLE VINCENT

COULD BE SINGLETONS AS

FOCAL POINTS OR IN TERRIFIC

GROUPS IN ANY GARDEN,

WHETHER TRADITIONAL OR

CONTEMPORARY.

WHEN BLUE IS THE MAIN

COLOUR (OPPOSITE), DON'T

OUR FRENCH COUSINS SAY *EN*

BLEU? VINCENT HAS PLAYED

MANY VARIATIONS ON THE

COLOUR IN HER GARDEN.

Half Acre

BOSCASTLE, CORNWALL

Carole Vincent

'The whole garden is a sculpture, isn't it? Even from the initial drawing stages, it was conceived as a complete piece of sculpture.'

Carole Vincent on Half Acre

Carole Vincent has lived in Boscastle for more than forty years. This is a very traditional part of Cornwall, and a surprising place to find a very contemporary garden, but there has been a significant artists' colony only a little way away in St Ives since the nineteenth century. It was founded by James Whistler and Walter Sickert, and the two most important sculptors to live in St Ives were Naum Gabo and Dame Barbara Hepworth. Carole Vincent knew Dame Barbara slightly, and admits that Hepworth's work, with its use of long sweeping curves, circles and very simple shapes, is often in her mind when she is designing her concrete sculptural objects. Her house and garden over-

look the harbour, which makes a great sinuous curve around the sea. This, as well as the other shapes of the Cornish landscape, have always been very important to her. For many years Carole Vincent was a figurative sculptor and she also taught dance, so she has great sensitivity for rhythm and movement.

Carole Vincent first started playing with concrete as a child, because her father was a builder who made concrete blocks. Even then she was impressed by how flexible it was as a building material, and how strong and durable. Her obsession with concrete re-emerged in the early 1980s, when she started experimenting with changing the colour and texture of the material. Traditionally, concrete is made in a limited range of shades, from very pale to dark grey and occasionally cream or gold, but Carole Vincent found that, by selecting certain dyes and pigments and mixing them with other substances now secret to her, she could create a full spectrum of colours in concrete, going from the very pale to the dark. With this in mind, she started making objects out of coloured concrete, sometimes using single colours and sometimes stratifying them.

For the millennium, she produced a very thin concrete cone in striated layers of many colours, which is sited in an amphitheatre in the castle grounds at Bude, in Cornwall. The cone is 9m (30ft) high, with a pinnacle of light at the top, and weighs 6 tons. The Bude Light sits on a great circle of coloured concrete tiles and comes alive after dark, when fibre optics light the patterns of the constellations twinkling in the zodiac circle at its base.

Recently, Carole Vincent has designed and installed a series of coloured concrete circles in the lower area of her garden. Two of these are ponds, one above the other, which interconnect. The whole of the garden is based on circles and squares (the measurements belong to the Fibonacci Sequence, where each number is equal to the sum of the preceding two numbers, i.e. 1, 1, 2, 3, 5, 8, 13 and so on). Much of the concrete is in a brilliant shade of blue, reflecting the colour of the adjacent sea on a very fine summer's day, but the blues vary where they become walls or supports for the concrete balls and columns that are also elements within this garden. The obelisks, cones and the tall square columns are all stratified with various colours, but often with a blue background. They are amazingly effective as garden sculptures. The coloured concrete balls can be very small in diameter, and the standing objects vary between 1m (3ft) and 9m (10ft), making these exciting sculptural forms suitable for any garden, however large or small.

Carole Vincent has deliberately chosen a background of plants which are evergreen, so that the garden is 'punctuated by the little flashes of colour that you get in brightly coloured concrete' seen against a green base. In the summer, a few colourful flowers such as geraniums or busy Lizzies in very bright pinks are allowed to decorate the garden for a few months, adding an extra spark. It is an extraordinarily contemporary garden, and a brilliant reminder that we are now in the twenty-first century ⚘

MAGIC DOOR (RIGHT) IS AN
ENTRANCE INTO SOME
WONDERLAND WITH THE DOOR
LEANING AGAINST FRAME. A SKY
PAINTED DISC IS EMBRACED BY
GOLDEN HOPS.
THE PRIMEVAL THREE LADIES,
GODDESSES, GRACES, FACES OF
EVE (REALLY DEPARTMENTAL
STORE DUMMIES)
MYSTERIOUSLY SCREENED BY
VIGOROUS MISCANTHUS. IVAN
HICKS HAS MAGRITTE-ISED
THEM WITH SKY AND CLOUDS
MAKE-UP.

ONE OF NINE AREAS
(OVERLEAF) IN HICKS' DESIGN,
AND HERE HE COMBINES THE
OBJETS TROUVÉS OR FOUND
OBJECTS WITH SPLENDIDLY
CLIPPED TOPIARY – SURREALISM
MEETS TRADITIONAL IN
SCULPTURAL CONTRAST.

Garden in Mind

STANSTEAD PARK, ROWLANDS CASTLE, HAMPSHIRE

Ivan Hicks

'Nature becomes a part in the making of sculpture because sometimes the found objects on their own don't look particularly exciting, and nature improves so well on what you do. I like the quote from André Breton, the high priest of Surrealism: "the marvellous that precipitate desire", the ability of the found object to liberate the artistic imagination.'

Ivan Hicks on Garden in Mind

Ivan Hicks grew up in south London just after the end of the Second World War and as a child he loved exploring the deserted gardens of nearby houses that had been bombed. The gardens were full of buddleias and a few other plants that struggled through a mass of weeds and ruins. In retrospect, he realises it was his introduction to the surreal world which he came to know better when he went to work as Edward James's gardener at the West Dean estate in Sussex in 1974.

Edward James became a patron of European surreal artists as early as the 1930s, and was one of the most significant collectors of surreal art. He was the first major patron of Salvador Dali, and between them they concocted the lobster telephone sculpture and the sofa based on Mae West's lips. As well as working with James in the West Dean gardens, Ivan Hicks also helped in his gardens at Las Posas, the pools with a paradisiacal microclimate near the town of Xilitla, in north-eastern Mexico, a mere seven hours by car from the capital. Here James created about 150 surreal giant concrete plant and flower sculptures and pavilions over a 25-year period, employing 68 local workmen at a cost of $5–10 million (£3.5–7 million).

The experience of working with James over more than twenty years has greatly influenced Ivan Hicks' vision of the garden and the landscape. In the late 1980s he was asked to redesign the wooded landscape

surrounding Groombridge Place, near Tunbridge Wells in Kent, a formal seventeenth-century house which had been the location for Peter Greenaway's superb film, *The Draughtsman's Contract.* He installed a magical sculptural trail in the woods, with a settlement of small-scale wooden houses and dens of little forest people, the Groms, whom he invented for children of all ages. While searching for the Groms, visitors have enchanting but bewildering sculptural design tricks played on them. What is reflected in the mirror suspended from the low branch of that tree? Where did the murky water in the pool come from? Why is there a half-Cherokee gypsy lady outside her caravan talking on a mobile telephone? How long will it be before the visitor returns to the real world? These are similar to the questions asked of visitors to Las Posas.

Ivan Hicks' most personal garden was made in 1990 in an old walled garden, and is entered through a doorway in the wall. Then the labyrinth that is known as the Garden in Mind begins. It is the extraordinary product of a creative imagination constantly asking questions and giving different answers. Although not obvious to the visitor, there is a formal structure, centred round a main path with a great circle in the middle and a circle at the end. This main feature has other circles on either side, making nine in all, nine being one of the most magical numbers. Anybody visiting the garden is quite unaware of this symbolism, because of the way both plants and other sculptural materials are used.

A path leads through trees and shrubs to a circular excavated area in which there are certain found objects, or *objets trouvés*. The eye is led towards the great circle in which, when we visited, there was a boat containing five upright oars, a bust and coils of wire: all objects that had been thrown away or abandoned and then found by Ivan Hicks on his travels. He places them in a way that gives them a surreal and mythical connection. In the depths of the garden, in a final circular pool, are three discarded mannequins from an old C&A department store, painted blue and overpainted with clouds, as if mirroring the sky

above. Are they nymphs? Are they goddesses? Are they merely *objets trouvés*? They all become sculptural when Ivan Hicks places them in this garden. In one area there is a large mirrored disco ball, which turns out to be a present from his wife, bought when they were out shopping together. Hicks loves it because he found it, he didn't have to pay for it, and now it is in his garden.

Elsewhere there is an amazing circle of leylandii hedging, which has grown into a cylinder 6m (20ft) tall. It is large enough for someone to walk inside through a tiny doorway and look out of two very small windows into areas of the garden not viewed before and ripe for exploration. This tower is only one of the many variations on the topiary form in this garden.

Of all the gardens that we have been to, this is the one that makes us most aware of change. Ivan Hicks encourages change all the time and is constantly moving and adding objects. He is never without his secateurs so that he can cut back or reorganise an outbreak of nature which he wishes to alter or control. When people first come to visit, some of them imagine the area has been abandoned and that the gardeners will soon come and clean it up; once they have explored the garden they love it, whatever age they may be. Ivan Hicks hears the words 'enchanted' and 'enthralling' all the time. A ninety-year-old lady said that the vibes for her were tremendous, and a nine-year-old boy said, 'Mum, this can't be a garden, it's too much fun.'

At one time Ivan Hicks lived on the estate but now he only comes once a week to alter, change and maintain. He says that he still uses the garden as his laboratory and as his artist's studio, so wherever he may create his next surrealist garden, the Garden in Mind remains the centre of his work and mind for his surreal sculptural universe 🜨

WELCOME TO SALVADOR DALI'S FORMER GARDEN OFFICE! (OPPOSITE) WE DOUBT HIS FORMIDABLE WIFE, GALA, WOULD HAVE TYPED OUT HIS DICTATION HERE.

HUMPTY DUMPTY (RIGHT)
IS THE FIRST SITE-SPECIFIC
SCULPTURE IN THE WOODS
AT GARDENS OF GAIA.
IN A CLEARING IN PETER
BARTLETT'S WOODLAND
SCULPTURE COLLECTION IS
RING OF HOPE.

Gardens of Gaia

CRANBROOK, KENT

Peter Bartlett

'What I love to see is people come in here quite stressed and leave with a totally new perspective, very relaxed.'
Peter Bartlett on Gardens of Gaia

Peter Bartlett started exploring the woodlands at Buckhurst Farm in Kent that have become the Gardens of Gaia as a child in the early 1950s. Even then he was fascinated by the light filtering through the trees and the stream that led through the woods to the lake. He has an artistic background, and at much the same time as he wanted to create his own sculpture park, he was given control of the sinuous 9 hectares (22 acres) of woodland that he has dedicated to Gaia. This is the Greek name for the Earth goddess who is responsible for all the earth's processes, including the way the natural landscape looks and changes millennium by millennium.

The woods are now home to a number of permanent sculptures, large and small, all made by people Peter Bartlett knows quite well. He invites them to come to the woods and spend as long as they like walking through them, watching the changing light and experiencing their sensations in this space. During this process they choose a site that inspires a sculpture which is placed on that site.

This process of making and placing sculpture in a naturalistic setting is based on the latest idea for planning any garden, which is called site-specific or site-generated. Before planning begins, a complete analysis of the site is made, and the information gathered dictates the design of the garden that is installed. It is the most important advanced theory and practice to emerge from the last two decades of the twentieth century. Practitioners include Kathryn Gustafson, who designed the ground plan at the National Botanic Garden of Wales, George Hargreaves, the head of

Landscape Architecture at Harvard University, and the many landscape designers trained at the Versailles School of Landscape Architecture. The amazing canyon garden at the Getty Art Centre, designed by the great American artist, Robert Irwin, is one example. This theory of landscape architecture has a parallel in site-specific sculpture, where analysis of the landscape precedes the making of the sculpture. The woods have been undisturbed for a very long time because they are on rocky, uneven terrain that could never be used for farming, and the sensations aroused by walking through these ancient woodlands determine the form and placing of their sculptures.

Many trees came down in the great storm of 1987, creating a series of vistas and a great deal more light. Peter Bartlett has done a little more clearing since then, and has made a couple of paths that lead from the entrance to the furthest point of the woods, where there is a lake, and back again, so most people walking through the woods will see most of the sculptures. The whole circuit takes about three-quarters of an hour to

complete. At the beginning of the walk, the lake seems a long way away, but for some reason the return journey appears to take much less time.

There are now about thirteen sculptures in the woods and there is always a temporary exhibition, which added another twelve pieces on the day we were there. The very first sculpture along the path is an enormous bloated form, of uncertain shape and material. It is designed by Alan Franklin and made of wood, but wood used in such a way that it appears to be solid, though in fact it is only a skin. It is called *Humpty Dumpty* and all the triangular pieces of wood have been joined so as to give the illusion of having been broken and then reconstructed.

In a slight clearing in the woods is Rip Kirby's *Ring of Hope*. This looks like a worn-out gazebo, made of rusting steel, but where its roof should be are images of five women, dancing in a crouched position around the top of the building; they too are made of rusting steel. Lime trees have been planted around the steel supports and one day the ladies will be dancing on top of a series of leafy green arches. This sculpture has antecedents in the gazebos that were used as focal points in rich men's gardens, but the ladies perched on top add a totally unexpected element.

As that fantastical image is lost to view, the spectacle of water that is the lake is suddenly glimpsed to one side of the woodland. Almost at its furthest end is the *Kissing Archway*, a sculpture of a man and woman kissing while facing each other with intertwined arms so that their bodies form an arch. It is constructed of very strong fibreglass which in certain lights makes the figures look as though they are made of marble. The arch is placed over a narrow stream next to the lake and, when the lake rises, the water may come up to their waists or even a little higher. Perhaps they are celebrating their chance meeting in the woods.

Out in the lake there is a figure of a crouching or squatting man made of rusting steel apparently floating on the surface. He never moves and is called the

Guardian of the Lake. In classical times all woods were dedicated to demi-gods, such as Dionysus or Pan, and remembering ancient mythology helped the sculptor decide on this piece.

On the return journey to the entrance of the gardens, some of the sculptures are deliberately made of materials that merge into the trees and only reveal themselves as the sun and light changes. There are five 6m (20ft) high circles, made of pieces of well-seasoned timber found in the woods, and set on the diagonal so that they are simultaneously seen and not seen. Their greyish-silvery colour fools the eye in the woodland light, making the thin, giant circles merge with their surroundings. One line of vision draws the eye through the circles and frames another sculpture in the distance.

Everybody's impressions of visiting the woods dedicated to Gaia are different. Some people laugh, and others cannot understand the path, but most are simply very impressed. Peter Bartlett hopes to 'open people's eyes to nature a bit more and to natural forms, not just the sculptures'; he thinks that, 'by placing sculptures in nature, it heightens people's perceptions. They look that bit more closely at what's around them.' He seems to have succeeded, for whenever he or the guardian walk through the woods, they find that visitors have placed a few twigs together, reorganised some stones, or found a trail of ivy and made their own temporary sculptures. Seeing these may inspire other visitors to do something similar in their own patch of ground

THE SPLENDIDLY SERENE

METAL SCULPTURE,

THE GUARDIAN OF THE LAKE.

(OPPOSITE AND ABOVE)

6 plants

The plant is, to the landscape artist, not only a plant –

rare, unusual, ordinary or doomed to disappearance – but it is also a colour, a shape,

a volume or an arabesque in itself.

Roberto Burle Marx

ome years ago, we wrote a book on the contemporary private garden throughout the world. The New York critics said it was wonderfully inspiring but some of the gardens had so few plants that, in the words of one reviewer, it was not only the most gorgeous garden porn but also 'post-plant'. Of course, plants do finally make a garden but we think they are just *one* element of many in the contemporary garden.

In many people's minds, there are only two sorts of garden. One is the cottage garden, with a path that leads from the garden gate to the front door. There are roses climbing over the house, and the garden on either side of the path has vegetables planted in neat rows or cottage garden flowers such as marigolds, wallflowers and sweet peas that grow easily and unassumingly amongst the vegetables.

The other sort of garden has a perennial border. It is assumed that this border has foliage and colour for eight months of the year and is flat, drab and dormant during winter. Such borders were originally inspired by William Robinson, as a contrast to the regimented, formal parterres. Robinson wrote many books, but his most important were *The Wild Garden* (1870) and *The English Flower Garden* (1883). He and Gertrude Jekyll were great friends and colleagues, and nowadays the herbaceous border is usually associated with Gertrude Jekyll. If herbaceous borders are to be successful they need to be contained and replanted on a very regular basis.

The brilliant plantpersons from Canada, Nori and Sandra Pope, are an inspiration if your cravings for the perfect garden can only be satisfied with a contemporary perennial border. Their borders in the old walled kitchen garden at Hadspen, Somerset, are full of perennials, but they have been used to create the most wonderful colour spectrum. Each of the partners has made a unique border, based on their vast and broad knowledge, choosing plants that flower for quite long periods during the year and often using the same species repeated in different colours.

Beth Chatto in Essex has a more practical approach, for she grows her plants on some of the most inhospitable soil that we have come across anywhere. Half the garden is fine gravel and sand, another area is clay, and a third is dry shade. Her philosophy is that you should choose plants that are naturally adapted to the growing conditions of the site and will thrive there without undue care and attention. Mrs Chatto has made the technique into an art.

Ivan Hicks, Britain's most successful surrealist gardener, has an amazing knowledge of plants but is equally happy when the winds blow seeds into his gardens so that whatever is planted is enhanced by Nature and her whims. There is a huge diversity of plants available today, whether annuals for colour or the new perennials in the form of the many fashionable grasses, and there is a renewed interest in exotics such as canna lilies and hardy bananas, spearheaded by the plantsman Christopher Lloyd. Let those people who are obsessed with a particular species collect as many as they wish, but we suggest that the rest of us simply choose plants that we like, that grow easily in our gardens, that need to be tamed and trimmed only occasionally and which give colour and scent during those times of the year when they will be most enjoyed 🌱

SQUARES OF LAWN AND SUCCULENT ANNUAL SEMPERFLORENS BEGONIA ARE THE BOLD DESIGN OF THE CHECKERBOARD GARDEN, PORT LYMPNE, KENT (PREVIOUS PAGE); A MUCH-USED, EVEN CLICHÉD, PLANT CAN BE USED WELL AND SPECTACULARLY.

CANAS AND BANANAS (OPPOSITE) IN EXOTIC GARDEN, GREAT DIXTER, EAST SUSSEX.

LARGE-SCALE LEAVES OF THE
PAULOWNIA TREE (RIGHT), ONE
OF MANY DRAMATIC PLANTS
THE POPES USE AS
COUNTERPOINT TO COLOUR
SPECTRUM DESIGNS.
ALLÉE OF LIME TREES
UNDERPLANTED ENCHANTINGLY
WITH HOSTAS – ANOTHER
DESIGN STROKE BY NORI AND
SANDRA POPE.

Hadspen Garden and Nursery

CASTLE CARY, SOMERSET

Sandra and Nori Pope

Hadspen House is a fine classical eighteenth-century house, built in the wonderful local golden Ham stone and allegedly paid for with profits from the slave trade. Its gardens are a typical story of attention and decay, followed by resurrection and further decay before their current incarnation. The most recent cycle begins in the early 1960s, when a member of the Hobhouse family, who had owned the house since the eighteenth century, married a keen gardener called Penelope. She used the gardens at Hadspen for her personal delight and as a laboratory for the ideas that made her a world-renowned plantswoman and garden designer.

Penelope Hobhouse has a more far-sighted view of garden design than is usual in Great Britain, but even she was influenced in her later designs by the time she spent at Tintinhull House in Somerset, where there are many herbaceous borders. The British enthusiasm for perennial borders had been redefined after the war because of the problems of maintenance, but Penelope Hobhouse and other ladies of her kind continued to write about these borders in the last decades of the twentieth century, thus encouraging many English gardeners to create gardens of nostalgia rather than innovation.

During Penelope Hobhouse's time at Hadspen, the large kitchen garden was used by a very skilful plant breeder called Eric Smith. She left, he left, and in 1987 a Canadian couple called Nori and Sandra Pope arrived from Vancouver Island and rented the 2 hectare (5 acre) kitchen garden from Niall Hobhouse. The Popes' brilliance has been to make everyone look at perennial plants in a different and much more imaginative way. Nori Pope was originally a graphic designer, so he knew how colours could be mixed and matched and when contrast is a good idea and when not, while Sandra Pope

NORI POPE'S PAIR OF
EXQUISITE WHITE, CREAM AND
YELLOW BORDERS (LEFT).
VENERABLE BRICK WALLS
(OPPOSITE) HARMONISE
BEAUTIFULLY WITH SANDRA
POPE'S VIVID BORDER OF RED,
PLUM AND PEACH.

had gained considerable horticultural experience on Vancouver Island. At Hadspen they had a palette on which they could combine their enthusiasm and knowledge.

They divided the main walled garden area into two borders, one for each of them. The planting in Sandra Pope's border, which is a great semicircle enclosed by the garden wall, goes through a magnificent range of colour from orange, red, yellow, plum, pink, peach and finally to deeper yellow. The effect she achieves is miraculous and inspiring. Sandra says, 'I have always been obsessed with colour and particularly mono-chrome colours, colours that harmonise together. I am not enthralled by contrast. I like colours that are subtle and work together.' She knows this amazing colour spectrum has to be in flower for six months of the year, when the garden is open to the public, and she has found that plants like the herbaceous potentillas in a

variety of colours (red, plum, yellow and apricot) are extremely useful, as are hemerocallis and asphodels. She uses many bulbs in the spring, favouring tulips in particular, and plants michaelmas daisies for late summer.

Nori Pope's pair of borders run down the slope at a right angle to the garden wall, culminating in a lime walk which leads to a hill that rises steeply from the main garden. A statue can be glimpsed halfway up the slope. He grows all the shades of white, cream and yellow, and he chose this area because the sun rises on one end of the border and sets on the other: the pale yellow plants look brilliant in the early morning sun and have an amber glow as the sun is setting. He too uses many tulips in the spring, with a wide range of euphorbias, going from pale almost to chartreuse, throughout the summer, and a collection of many different hostas in the shade of the beech walk. For Nori

Pope, 'Influences are many, but they come particularly from painting. Take Georges Braque's *Picnic*, and its contrasting shadows. I think, If I put ajuga under an orange azalea, it will look fantastic and there will be a shadow effect. Great paintings are all about illusion, and these optical illusions can be created with plants.'

I HAVE ALWAYS BEEN OBSESSED WITH COLOUR AND PARTICULARLY MONOCHROME COLOURS, COLOURS THAT HARMONISE TOGETHER.

Both Sandra and Nori Pope try out different plants every year and are ruthless about disposing of the ones that do not flower or grow satisfactorily. They are as obsessed with new and different plants as any true plant collector, but they also know that they have established their reputation with their brilliant colour schemes and

that is why they are so meticulous about constantly changing the plants they use. One of their most successful innovations is to repeat the same plant in different colours through a border.

The six months when the gardens are not open are spent clearing up, planting and replanting so that there will be another amazing display when the season starts again at Easter. They are very much a hands-on couple and have only one full-time assistant working for them. They have a nursery where some but not all of the plants in the borders can be bought, but they do not do mail order: should you wish to do a variation on their brilliant borders using their plants, you have to go to this enchanted garden in Somerset. But once there, you will be thrilled and overwhelmed by the spectrum of colours, made up of plants brilliantly chosen. Now in its fourth creation, the old kitchen garden is probably more beautiful than ever before 🌱

PHILIP SASSOON'S GUESTS
ENJOYED A SPECTACULAR
SWIMMING POOL; NOW THE
WATER REFLECTS THE SKY
(RIGHT).

THE FABULOUS VIEW
(OPPOSITE) FROM PORT LYMPNE
OUT ACROSS THE ROMNEY
MARSHES TO THE CHANNEL –
THE MAIN REASON SIR PHILIP
SASSOON BUILT PORT LYMPNE.

Port Lympne
HYTHE, KENT
Russell Page

At the beginning of the twentieth century, a very rich young man called Sir Philip Sassoon had a fantasy that became Port Lympne. His family originated in the Middle East and India and were fabulously rich traders and merchants who became anglicised. He was determined that his mansion with its surrounding gardens would truly astonish all his guests, however grand and pretentious they might be, so he employed the well-known architect, Sir Herbert Baker. (He had worked with Sir Edwin Lutyens for some years before they fell out about the major avenue within their joint project, building New Delhi.)

Baker succeeded magnificently at Port Lympne, creating a spectacular garden from which there is a view over Romney Marshes to the Channel and occasionally on fine days even across to the coast of France. Because the house and garden are on a hill, the area below the house had to be terraced. The central feature, three terraces down, was a large pool with jets of water. Only the central square area with its jet remains, and it is still the eye-catcher for the entire garden vista. Elsewhere, there is a wonderful rhododendron walk with a statue at one end. From there, the very impressive Trojan Steps, edged with yew, lead down to the main level of the gardens.

The gardens fell into decay after Sir Philip's death in 1939 and the restoration only started when John Aspinall bought Lympne in 1973. At that time he contacted Russell Page, who came to advise on the replanning of some parts of the garden. Sir Philip Sassoon certainly knew Russell Page when he was a young man in the 1930s and would also have known many of Russell Page's clients, but there is no record that he actually helped design any of the gardens at that time. Aspinall wished to re-create the garden Sassoon had built, including the two rectangular areas seen from the main terrace: the Checkerboard Garden and the Striped Garden.

These areas are partly enclosed by softly battle-mented yew hedges, and planted out with annuals. Both are an interesting way of using colour in the garden, and the plant material and colours can be changed annually according to whim. The Checkerboard Garden (which consists of five rows of seven squares, planted in alternate blocks of red and white, separated by squares of lawn) is usually planted with two different colours of small-flowered begonias, which last longer and are easier to maintain than the large-flowered varieties. It is still, however, a labour-intensive area because of the difficulty of mowing the grass areas between the flower squares.

The Striped Garden (which has three long, narrow beds) has gone through various re-creations. Originally it was planted with stripes of *Calendula*, the old English marigold, but now contains French and African marigolds. These species need a little less maintenance and give a controlled coloured effect. In 1986 it was laid out as a Persian Carpet with *Ageratum* 'Bluebird', *Lobelia* 'Crystal Palace' and white *Impatiens*, the ever-popular busy Lizzie. At different times the marigolds have been bordered with silver leaf or lobelias. Inevitably, the plants chosen for a bedding scheme like this must be fairly neat in habit and should be in flower for at least three months. Provided the bed is very closely planted, there is little weeding to do, and the bed will look decorative for a considerable part of the summer. But do not mix too many colours or the scheme will start to resemble an unimaginative municipal planting.

Below the main level of the garden is another area on which there are four terraces. One is laid out as a bowling green; the other three are filled with dahlias, roses or herbaceous plants. On the day we visited, the dahlia border was as magnificent as any we have ever seen. The flowers ranged in size from small to very large and made a wonderful shock of colour. It was a triumph of garden maintenance. Sir Philip Sassoon always wanted his gardens to look their best in August, when he preferred to be *en residence*, and I think his shadow would have been delighted with the dahlia terrace at that moment ❧

MONUMENTAL TROJAN STEPS (OPPOSITE) DESIGNED BY SIR HERBERT BAKER IN COLLABORATION WITH CLIENT, SASSOON; THE YEW HEDGES HAVE BEEN RE-PLANTED.
NOEL COWARD WOULD JUST POSSIBLY HAVE DESCRIBED THIS DAHLIA BORDER AS 'AN IRRITANT TO THE RETINA' (RIGHT), BUT THESE SMALLER FORMS CAN BE FLOWER ARRANGERS' DELIGHT.

A DOWN VIEW TO IVAN
HICKS' FRAME GARDEN (RIGHT)
TIMES TWO. ONE: THE YELLOW
PICTURE FRAMES IN THE CENTRE
OF THE BOARD WALK BEDDING
DESIGN AND TWO: ENTIRE BED
FRAMED WITH MARIGOLDS.
THE GARDEN DESIGNER'S
FRAMING TECHNIQUE PUSHED
TO SURREAL EDGE WITH
PICTURE FRAMES (OPPOSITE)
FOCUSING VIEWS OUT TO THE
HARBOUR AT GOSPORT,
HAMPSHIRE.

Framed Planting

GOSPORT, HAMPSHIRE

Ivan Hicks

'I was asked to create a flower border on any theme I wanted. So I thought, Why not treat the whole thing as a picture? The idea of using actual picture frames as vertical elements gave so many possibilities for people looking to frame various views.'

Ivan Hicks on Framed Planting

In the last decade municipal planting has been increasingly reviled as the gardening *cognoscenti* say that it has nothing to do with contemporary horticulture and design. It is true that much municipal planting is quite high maintenance, needing to be replanted two or three times a year as well as requiring regular watering and weeding. But it can have a charming mass appeal. The dark grass and plane tree reservation down the centre of Park Lane in central London has been replaced with raised beds of tulips and wallflowers, succeeded by plantings of phormium among masses of varicoloured busy Lizzies, to cheer motorists stuck in a traffic jam. Municipal mind-sets are slowly changing, and a few examples of some of the most extravagant civic planting are still to be found each year in the great marquees at the Chelsea Flower Show.

In 2001, Southern Arts asked Ivan Hicks to design a garden in an area approximately 2m (6ft) wide and 18m (60ft) long by the edge of the harbour at Gosport. It is overlooked by a twenty-storey block of flats and bordered by a row of council houses. In the distance, Nelson's flagship *Victory* can be seen in Portsmouth Harbour. Ivan Hicks pondered this rather unprepossessing space and decided to plant it out as a formal parterre, using bright marigolds around the edge, infilled with blue ageratums.

Such a design could have been planted at any time over the last 150 years, but the difference here is that

there are three large yellow picture frames, approximately 1m (3ft) wide by 2m (6ft) high, standing in the parterre. The detail on each frame is slightly different but is reproduced on both sides, so that the view is

FRAMING THE VIEW IS A BASIC SKILL OF ALL LANDSCAPE AND GARDEN DESIGNERS, AND HAS BEEN BROUGHT UP TO DATE IN A VERY CLEVER AND LITERAL WAY IN THIS GOSPORT MUNICIPAL BORDER.

framed correctly no matter how you look through the frames. The marigold edging of the bed can in turn be thought of as a horizontal frame for the frames. What a witty idea, beautifully realised.

Some of the local people were at first astonished and horrified by what they were looking at, but as time passed they began to understand the game that Ivan

Hicks is playing. He wanted to make the viewer understand that any planted area can be viewed from an incredible number of different angles and perspectives. Framing the view is a basic skill of all landscape and garden designers, and has been brought up to date in a very clever and literal way in this Gosport municipal border. One of the frames magically outlines the *Victory* at one moment, then frames a ship passing out of the harbour to the English Channel. Another frame contains a view of the council blocks or, from a different point of view on the other side, a passerby enjoying a walk on the new contemporary walkway that looks down on to the harbour scene. It is, of course, an artist's installation and may disappear by the end of the year, but momentarily it makes everybody who passes look at the garden in a different way

MISCANTHUS AND BANANA

PLANTS (RIGHT) ARE BUT TWO

OF THE VIVID SUBJECTS CHOSEN

TO BE IN THE NEWISH EXOTIC

GARDEN AT GREAT DIXTER.

END OF THE SEAMLESS

LONG BORDER AT GREAT DIXTER

(OPPOSITE) AND THE ARTS AND

CRAFTS EXTENSION, HOME OF

THE LLOYD FAMILY, DESIGNED

BY THE GREAT ARCHITECT, SIR

EDWIN LUTYENS.

THE EXOTIC GARDEN

(OVERLEAF) IN ALL ITS VIBRANT

GLORY.

Great Dixter

RYE, EAST SUSSEX

Christopher Lloyd

'If you are not interested, obviously you want [a garden] to be low maintenance, but then you don't get much thrill from what you've done. And I think every plant and every scene should give you a bit of a buzz.'
Christopher Lloyd on Great Dixter

Christopher Lloyd was born at Great Dixter in 1921, nine years after his parents moved into the house. It had been enlarged for them by Sir Edwin Lutyens, who also helped with the design of the gardens. When the formal gardens were first laid out, Lutyens suggested that the windbreaks and divisions within the garden should be walls made of brick or stone. Christopher Lloyd's father, knowing the cost of such construction, suggested they should be made of yew instead and it is yew hedges that still divide one area from another, though they need considerable annual maintenance.

His mother was an obsessed gardener and it was she who persuaded Lutyens that there should be not only a formal garden but also informal meadow areas beside the driveway to the house and between the high-maintenance areas of the garden and the surrounding landscape. Some people think the wild meadow areas, through which grass paths are mown, have been added to the gardens recently so as to reduce the amount of maintenance, but they have always been there, and nearby four trees that his parents inherited: a laurel, a wild pear, a yew and a mulberry tree.

The gardens that we see today were originally his mother's domain, but Christopher Lloyd would leave copious notes for her each week about things that he considered should be done in the garden while he was away teaching at Wye College. He would usually find these tasks completed when he returned at the weekend. As he became well known, both as a weekly

contributor to *Country Life* and the author of an enormous number of books on gardening, so the fortunes of Great Dixter changed. It has become a garden visited by thousands of people, many of whom buy plants from his nursery at the end of their visit. This means that there are now sufficient funds for a staff of six during the summer and five during the winter, looking after the high-maintenance gardens and the nursery. The gardens are now the joint vision of Christopher Lloyd and his head gardener, Fergus Garrett.

Christopher Lloyd is quite unashamed about the high maintenance, particularly of the Peacock and Topiary areas of the garden and his very famous Long Border. He experiments with these areas every year. Some of the plants were chosen by his mother decades ago, but others are changed because he wishes to alter the colours or the contrasting leaf shapes, or because one group of plants that he is trying out has done spectacularly well. His view is that nothing is sacred, and it is his eye and his memory that determine which plants should be kept and which replaced. There are no plans.

Two areas of the garden have been developed over the last ten years. The first is the Exotic Garden, where there was originally a formal rose garden. This was removed on Fergus's arrival and has now become an area of vibrant colour. There are dahlias and cannas and a haze of *Verbena bonariensis*, a hardy Japanese banana called *Musa basjoo* and, as a contrast, a wild flowering shrub, *Escallonia bifida*, which flowers in August and September and is covered in butterflies.

The other area, which has also become a mass of brilliant colour in August and September, is the Sunk Garden. Having been a vegetable garden during the First World War, this space was created by Christopher Lloyd's father in the early 1920s. The spoil from digging out the octagonal pool was used to fill in a pond on the other side of the garden. The pool is surrounded by a wide paving area with drystone walls against which very highly coloured, late-flowering plants and shrubs are now grown.

Christopher Lloyd says that gardens are all about the change of seasons; where possible there should be one area of your garden which looks wonderful in spring, another in high summer and a third in the autumn. With 2 hectares (5 acres) of gardens at Great Dixter, he has enough space to have such areas. With encouragement from Fergus and the necessity of writing about something new every week in *Country Life*, the gardens are always changing, even though their framework has been established since 1912. Christopher Lloyd's enthusiasm is considerable and this influential garden, which has spanned the whole of the twentieth century, continues to be a grand plantsman's vision at the beginning of the second millennium 🌱

SUPERB MIXED PLANTINGS (OPPOSITE) AT GREAT DIXTER.

TOPIARY GARDEN (BELOW) DESIGNED BY CHRISTOPHER LLOYD'S FATHER.

BIRCH TREES (RIGHT)
CHARMINGLY EMBRACED BY
IVY RESCUED FROM DENSE
UNDERGROWTH, AND NO,
IT WILL NOT KILL THE TREES,
COUNTER TO CURRENT
OPINION.

WILD GARDEN CREATED FROM
FORMER FARM FIELDS WITH
NATURALISTIC POND AS THE
CENTRAL FEATURE. IT WAS
ALL DESIGNED BY JULIE TOLL,
A LEADING BRITISH GARDEN
DESIGNER.

Jenningsbury Farm
HERTFORDSHIRE
Julie Toll

'The wild [plant] fits so well with the contemporary; it softens it. You see so many people trying to be modern for the sake of it and it doesn't sit in the setting, but I think the wild and the contemporary can really complement each other very well.'

Julie Toll on Jenningsbury Farm

It must have been some time in the 1980s that the idea of a wild flower meadow started being noised abroad again in gardening articles. Christopher Lloyd's mother had planted wild flower meadows at Great Dixter in the early part of the twentieth century, having been influenced by William Robinson's work, but the name now most frequently connected with such wild flower plantings is that of Miriam Rothschild, who swept away the family gardens around her house in Cambridgeshire and replaced them in 1970 with a wild flower meadow.

Julie Toll made her name by winning a Gold Medal at the Chelsea Flower Show with a wild flower meadow in 1993. She had been somewhat apprehensive about showing such a garden at Chelsea, thinking many of the judges would look at the plants and say they were nothing but weeds. We know that weeds are plants that have yet to find their use, or worse, plants that have grown in the wrong place, but the main problem with a wild flower meadow is that it takes a great deal of planning, and much more importantly, a great deal of patience and hard work.

Many people have the mistaken idea that anyone with a piece of land can make a wild flower meadow, simply by buying a few packets of wild flower seed and sprinkling them around in the early spring. Then, lo and behold, a wild flower meadow appears from May to August, only needing to be mown once, and that is all the maintenance it takes. The truth is quite different!

(We know a wild flower meadow in the depths of Gloucestershire that is only cut once a year in late August; everything else in the meadow is left to chance. After a full twenty-five years of chance, it is now quite an agreeable area to look at for two or three months of the year...)

Most people do not have the time, the tolerance or the patience to wait entirely for Nature. Julie Toll knows this, and over the years she has learnt several things about this type of gardening. Ideally, the soil should not be too fertile because this encourages wild native grasses to strangle and suffocate the lesser breeds of desired plants: wild flowers. These bloom at different times of the season and you may have to decide whether you want a spring, summer or late-summer meadow. The choice of wild flowers and the time at which the meadow is mown will both be different, depending on the preferred season. It also became very apparent to

Julie Toll that seeds do not produce the sort of wild flower meadow that people want and that plugs (wild flowers grown from seed in their first year of growth and transplanted) are a much more reliable way of achieving the desired effect. They also allow a greater diversity of plant choice, colour and leaf shape. Finally, wild flowers do not thrive when planted singly and must be grown in clumps or drifts.

Having retired from farming, the owners of Jenningsbury Farm came to Julie Toll with about 3 hectares (8 acres) of land around the house which needed some attention. Three-quarters of the land was surrounded by a moat that had been there for a thousand years, they added a small pond, shaded by some lovely old willow trees. The rest of the site was flat, bare grassland which had been grazed as pasture. Whatever she did, the owners hoped it would be attractive for a very considerable period of the year and that it would be

some areas appeared entirely bare or bloomed with species that had not been expected, and the grass paths needed to be mown every week. But slowly the owners became obsessed with their new garden. Now they have a maintenance gardener five days a week and a wild flower expert who comes once a month. Julie Toll is on call whenever necessary. They realise that all this time and effort is necessary if they are to have the wild flower landscape of their dreams.

Eight years on, in late summer, there were tall grasses and mature wild flowers swaying in the breeze, and the mown paths encouraged exploration of the various areas on the circuit through the landscape. The rushes and willows around the enlarged pond, to say nothing of the water lilies, made us want to walk across the little bridge or sit on the edge and count the butterflies. The woods dividing the garden from the moat were dark and mysterious; their spring-flowering wild flowers had mainly reverted to green, and the trunks and branches of the trees were covered in a veil of ivy. A birch grove had recovered sufficiently from being choked with ivy to hide an unsightly neighbouring barn, and birds flew in and out, knowing they were safe.

If you want a wild flower meadow in your garden then, realistically, the garden must be large enough for people to come upon it unexpectedly, enjoy it for a few months of the year and then ignore it after the inevitable mowing until the following spring. But if your garden is small or you only have a balcony, a wild flower pot with just a few different wild flower species (heartsease, silver weed and ragged robin, for example) will look pretty. The wild flower pot is Julie Toll's suggestion and she really does know what she is doing

low maintenance, as they were looking forward to a larger choice of activities in their retirement.

None of this happened. Julie Toll planned a completely naturalistic design, which required a lot of maintenance. She decided that some areas needed to be enclosed further so that there was a sequence of open and enclosed spaces; the pond would be enlarged; and there had to be paths leading through the various areas, which would almost certainly be made of mown grass. No budget was mentioned but she said that it was unlikely to look satisfactory in less than five years without greatly increasing the cost.

The owners slightly unwillingly agreed to all this, and were dismayed when Julie Toll had the meadow cut in the spring of year one in order to make the wild plant material more vigorous. She prepared the ground with weedkiller to get rid of the couch grass, had the larger pond dug and bridges built. For the first three years,

GLORIOUS MIXTURE OF WILD
GRASSES (OPPOSITE) WITH
MATURING SEEDHEADS TO BE
MOWED SOON AT
JENNINGSBURY FARM,
HERTFORDSHIRE.

SPLENDID CONTRASTING
PLANT GROUPING (RIGHT) BY
PIET OUDOLF, DUTCH GRASSES
EXPERT, FOR PLANTSMAN JOHN
COKE; VERTICAL FOXGLOVES
AND ALLIUMS COUNTERPOINT
THE HORIZONTAL MASS OF
DESCHAMPSIA GRASS.

Bury Court

FARNHAM, SURREY

John Coke

'People speak of new-wave perennial planting, but they are mostly old plants used in a new way. The colours are different, I think. Not the bright, clear colours of traditional herbaceous borders, but tawny, rusty, terracotta tones.'

John Coke on Bury Court

John Coke grew up at Jenkyn Place in Hampshire, just down the road from Bury Court, where his father created a very large but traditional garden over half a century. It was this that inspired him to become a horticulturist. More than twenty years ago he started a small nursery where he had a selection of unusual plants, both annual and perennial, some trees and a few shrubs: anything in fact that would attract a sufficient number of buyers to make it commercially viable. Fifteen years ago he moved to Bury Court because it was larger and it had an outer and inner yard. The inner yard, which was still a farmyard when he bought it, could be used as a sales area and show garden, and the outer could be used for growing and displaying plants.

Having known Piet Oudolf, the Dutch nurseryman and designer, for many years, John Coke has been converted to Oudolf's idea that perennial borders should look good for as long as possible during the year while also being naturalistically planted. (This is something of a contradiction in terms because cultivar perennials are not found growing in the wild.) For Oudolf, larger amounts of fewer species in a border can make the space more interesting. It no longer needs to be protected by a tall wall or a hedge, and shrubs are banished. Oudolf had long experimented with this idea in his own garden in Holland, although there is a surprising eye-catcher of tall, intercepting, triangular yew hedges at the furthest end of the garden. These seem to have also an aesthetic purpose, but also act as partial screening from the stormy Dutch weather.

The soil in the farmyard at Bury Court was pure rich greensand, which can grow a wide range of plants but needs considerable watering as it drains very quickly. In the borders John Coke has used classic perennials such as phloxes, asters and achilleas, planted in swaths, but has tended to choose colours which are not usually associated with each species. The use of perennial grasses in borders has made Piet Oudolf famous in Europe. He says they 'remind me of nature'. John Coke has found them highly effective in his own borders, and has chosen about five different varieties. Most of them are strong enough to grow upright for a long period during the year, though their colours may change at the beginning of winter, when many of them take on a gold rather than a brown hue. He is careful to keep them tidy, as he does with all the perennials in his borders, and some are staked because he realises the importance of differing scale in any border. He allows a few to remain until March, when they are cut down. Then the soil is fertilised and any reorganisation of the other perennial borders is done.

In mid-summer, the borders were looking wonderful but even he cannot resist some aspects of the traditional perennial border. He has built a 2m (6ft) high wall behind the longest border, so that the eye is focused on the border and not the adjacent landscape. Three groups of catalpas are placed to catch the eye as they come into flower and elsewhere some evergreen shrubs (box and yew) have been allowed. Beneath the catalpas there was a mist of gypsophila with a few red daisies growing through them, which made a different and quite unexpected tapestry in one area of the garden.

There is nothing more boring than a perennial garden that only uses grasses: it looks woebegone, untidy and melancholy for long periods of the winter; but the grasses in this garden are used to striking effect as a counterpoint to other perennials or evergreens. In one excellent pairing, a giant bed of feathery grasses contains a bronze foxglove, as a complete contrast. John Coke's display garden is a reminder of how important it is to understand the needs of perennial plants and to use them in big clumps or drifts, with maximum contrast wherever possible 🌿

STRONG SCULPTURAL CIRCLE OF BOXWOOD (LEFT) CONTRASTING WITH LAWN AND DENSE UNDERSTORY OF GRASSES IN BACKGROUND; IN THIS GARDEN, WE LEARNED HOW EFFECTIVE AND BEAUTIFUL GRASSES COULD BE.
BOUND CLUMPS OF GRASSES AS VERTICALS (OPPOSITE) TO STRONG HORIZONTALS OF GREY-LEAVED AND BLUE-FLOWERED PLANTINGS.

HABITAT IS EVERYTHING

TO THE GREAT PLANTS-

WOMAN, BETH CHATTO.

USING WILD PLANTS AS

ORNAMENTALS IS BUT ONE

OF HER SKILLS; (RIGHT)

PLANTS THAT THRIVE IN DRY

SHADE.

SUPERB PLANT

COMBINATIONS (OPPOSITE)

BASED ON HARMONY AND

MORE, CONTRAST BETWEEN

MATURE FORM AND LEAF

SHAPE; THE RESULTS ARE

STUNNING.

The Beth Chatto Gardens

COLCHESTER, ESSEX

Beth Chatto

'I start with shapes, textures, foliage, before flowers.'
Beth Chatto

Beth Chatto is considered the finest plants-woman in Great Britain. A major part of her planting philosophy involves taking advantage of plants' natural adaptation to particular habitats. She matches plants to a specific site only after careful analysis of the growing conditions, choosing species that would grow there naturally – and there is a wondrous diversity of plants available, no matter how difficult the site.

The Chatto family had owned a farm near Elmstead Market for quite a long time and Andrew Chatto, Beth Chatto's late husband, had known from a very early age that it would be his responsibility to look after the farm, which was mainly planted with a variety of fruit trees. In the early 1960s life changed dramatically. Much of

the farm, including the family house, was sold and Beth and Andrew Chatto moved to 1.62 hectares (4 acres) of land where almost nothing had ever been grown as it was considered waste ground. There was a shallow valley through which a stream trickled, keeping the area nearest to it moist or even soggy throughout most of the year, but above the valley was an area of dried-out

I START WITH SHAPES, TEXTURES, FOLIAGE, BEFORE FLOWERS.

clay gravel which had never been used for agricultural purposes. The entire area was an overgrown wilderness with 300-year-old oaks making dry shade. Moreover, this part of eastern England receives less than 50cm (20in) of rain a year.

It was here that the Chattos built a new house and Beth Chatto started to experiment with plants that

would grow in the extremely inhospitable situation. Even in those early days, her nursery was well known for growing unusual plants suitable for more difficult habitats: damp conditions, shade and partial shade gardens and dry gardens. When we first visited twenty-five years ago, her name was starting to be known in gardening circles. At that time we had a special interest in herbs, and we wanted to know which ones she considered to be drought-resistant.

In March 1992, Beth Chatto moved her car park and made a new dry garden, using her experience of almost forty years. The area is mainly gravel and sand, which hardly retains any water, and her method of dealing with such an inhospitable situation is to clear it of anything already there and then mulch it with organic compost, digging it in to a depth of approximately 30cm (12in). Mrs Chatto then places a layer of very fine gravel as 'icing', and plants a wide selection of many different species which will grow in such circumstances. These are generally drought-resistant natives of the Mediterranean. She plants big drifts of one type of plant,

which look much more effective than the 'dolly mixture' technique of one of everything.

Beth Chatto is quite ruthless about the way she maintains this area. After the first year, when the plants are watered by hand, the only water comes from the sky. There is no irrigation system and the plants are simply left to live or die, but the number and variety of plants that survive in these apparently inhospitable conditions is quite staggering. As Beth Chatto has said, 'The effect in the first summer of 1992 was very rewarding, despite several periods of drought. Bold shapes, textures and colours transformed the bare site into a welcoming garden in one brief summer.' Some of the plants are bulbs, such as scilla, crocus, chionodoxa and small wild tulips. Bergenia and euphorbia are successful, as are the grey-foliaged plants like ballota, lavender and santolina. Intrigued by the latest trend for grasses, she is growing a few in this dry area, but is still uncertain how decorative they are during their long dry period when they sway in the winter breeze.

In the Water Garden, through which the little stream once ran, two large ponds have been dug, approximately 2m (6ft) deep and lined with puddled clay. They are surrounded by plants that like being at the water's edge, such as marsh marigold, winter fern, swamp cypress, gunnera and 'tortured' willows. There are groups of water lilies in the pond. Beth Chatto brings the same philosophy to this garden as to the dry garden, so water-loving plants that become inundated and die are simply removed.

There are now patches through the wooded area where the trees have been thinned out, allowing sufficient light for shade-loving plants such as ferns, ivies and hostas. This area is enchanting,

with the dappled light coming through the leaves, and it contains a considerable range of shade-loving plants which appear to be self sown, but this is not the case. Once again, the plants that like such an environment are allowed to thrive and the others are dug up and discarded.

Mrs Chatto is brutal about disposing of the plant in the wrong place and she wishes that more gardeners would follow her example. For her, gardening is a learning process, in which you slowly find out which plants will do well in your particular conditions through a process of trial and error. Be ruthless with the ones that do not flourish and plant many more of the species that you like and that like your environment. Your knowledge will increase as you find plants that prosper under your tender care. We particularly like Beth Chatto's comments on garden maintenance. She says that a garden is like a child, so keeping it clean and fed and well cared for is a pleasure, and not a burden.

Forty years ago, Beth Chatto never imagined that she would achieve the success she has today. She is a superb plantswoman and listening to her story will encourage so many people to look again at the plants in their garden. Perhaps all those people who think they are not 'green fingered' and fear they will kill any plant they touch may even be persuaded by her example to have another go. She and her garden are truly inspirational

DAPPLED SHADE AREA (LEFT) WITH PLANTS CHOSEN BY BETH CHATTO, WHO CONSISTENTLY ACHIEVES HER IDEAL OF THE RIGHT PLANT IN THE RIGHT PLACE; THE RUSTIC BENCH IS PERFECTLY JUDGED HERE. **BETH CHATTO** MADE HER

BEAUTIFUL GARDEN (ABOVE) AGAINST ALL NATURE'S GIVENS, HERE IT'S DRY SHADE, DEEP GRAVEL ENRICHED WITH COMPOST AND THE NARROW DITCH STREAM SHE DAMMED AND TRANSFORMED INTO TWO CHARMING PONDS.

Select Bibliography
OF REFERENCES
AND RECOMMENDED FURTHER READING

GENERAL TRADITIONAL GARDENS

Amherst, The Hon. Alicia. *A History of Gardening in England.* Quaritch, London 1895

Bisgrove, Richard. *The National Trust Book of the English Garden.* Viking, London 1990

Brookes, John. (*All* of his Books on Design and Plants)

Coats, Peter. *Great Gardens of Britain.* Artus, London 1977

Crowe, Sylvia. *Garden Design. Country Life*, London 1965

Gothein, Marie Luise. *A History of Garden Art.* (2 vols.) J.M. Dent and Sons, London 1928

Hadfield, Miles, Robert Harling and Leonie Highton. *British Gardeners: A Biographical Dictionary*, Zwemmer and Conde Nast, London 1980

Hobhouse, Penelope. *Private Gardens of England.* Weidenfeld and Nicolson, London 1986

Hunt, John Dixon. *The Genius of the Place.* Elek, London 1975

Huxley, Anthony. *An Illustrated History of Gardening.* Paddington, London 1978

Huxley, Anthony and Mark Griffiths. *The New Royal Horticultural Society Dictionary of Gardening.* (4 vols.) Macmillan, London 1992

Hyams, Edward. *Capability Brown and Humphry Repton.* Scribners, New York 1970

Jellicoe, Geoffrey and Susan, Patrick Goode, Michael Lancaster. *The Oxford Companion to Gardens.* Oxford University Press, Oxford and New York 1986

Jellicoe, Geoffrey and Susan. *The Landscape of Man.* Thames and Hudson, London 1987

Strong, Roy and Julia Trevelyan Oman. *A Celebration of Gardens.* HarperCollins, London 1991

Tipping, H. Avray. *English Gardens. Country Life*, London 1925

GENERAL: CONTEMPORARY GARDENS

Adams, William Howard. *Denatured Visions: Landscape and Culture in the Twentieth Century.* Museum of Modern Art, New York 1991

Cooper, Guy and Gordon Taylor. *Paradise Transformed: The Private Garden for the Twenty-first Century.* The Monacelli Press, New York 1995

Cooper, Guy and Gordon Taylor. *Gardens for the Future: Gestures Against the Wild.* Conran Octopus, London 2000

Delaney, Topher. *Ten Landscapes.* Rockport Publishing, Gloucester, Massachusetts 2001

Domaine de Kerguehennec. *Catalogue of Site Specific Sculpture.* Brittany, France 1998

Eckbo, Garrett. *Garrett Eckbo: A Philosophy of Landscape.* Process Architecture: No. 90, Tokyo 1990

Holden, Robert. *International Landscape Design.* Laurence King Publishing, London 1996

Imbert, Dorothee. *The Modernist Garden in France.* Yale University Press, New Haven 1993

Jellicoe, Geoffrey and Susan, Patrick Goode and Michael Lancaster. *The Oxford Companion to Gardens*, Oxford and New York 1986

Karson, Robin. *Fletcher Steele, Landscape Architect: An account of a garden maker's life.* Abrams, New York 1989

Kassler, Elizabeth. *Modern Gardens and the Landscape.* Museum of Modern Art, New York 1964

Keeney, Gavin. *On the Nature of Things.* Birkhauser, Basel/Berlin/Boston 2000

Larsen, Jack Lenor. *A Weaver's Memoir.* Abrams Press, New York 1998

Lund, Annemarie. *A Guide to Danish Landscape Architecture 1000–1996.* Arkitektens Forlag, Copenhagen 1997

Pigeat, Jean-Paul. *Festival des Jardins* (Château de Chaumont near Tours, France Annual International Festival of Contemporary Gardens). Editions du Chene–Hachette Livre, Paris 1995

Spens, Michael. *Landscape Transformed.* Academy Editions, London 1996

Spirn, Anne Whiston. *The Language of Landscape.* Yale University Press, New Haven 1998

Treib, Marc. *Modern Landscape Architecture: A Critical Review.* The MIT Press, Cambridge, Mass 1998

Treib, Marc and Dorothee Imbert. *Garrett Eckbo: Modern Landscapes for Living.* University of California Press, Berkeley and Los Angeles 1997

Zacca, Frederica. *Luis Barragan: The Quiet Revolution.* Skira, Milan 2000

REFERENCES FOR SIX ELEMENTS OF GARDEN DESIGN
TIME

Earle, Alice Morse. *Sundials and Roses of Yesterday.* Macmillan, London 1902

Hay, Roy (Ed.). *The Gardening Year.* Reader's Digest, London 1968

Henslow, T. Geoffrey W. *Ye Sundial Booke* (Foreword: Beverley Nichols). Foyle, London 1935

Pavord, Anna. *The Flowering Year.* Chatto and Windus, London 1991

Richardson, Tim. Editor of *New Eden: The Contemporary Gardens Magazine*, IPC, London journal: 1999–2000

FORM

Beardsley, John. *Earthworks and Beyond: Contemporary Art in the Landscape.* Abbeville Press, New York 1998

Bourdon, David. *Designing the Earth: The human impulse to shape nature.* New York 1995

Celant, Germano. *Michael Heizer (Earthworks).* Fondazione Prada, Italy 1997

Cooper, Guy and Gordon Taylor. *Mirrors of Paradise: The Gardens of Fernando Caruncho.* The Monacelli Press, New York 2000

Herd, Stanley James. *Crop Art.* New York 1994

Irwin, Robert. *Retrospective Exhibition: 1993.* Catalogue. Museum of Contemporary Art. Los Angeles, California

Kiley, Dan and Jane Amidon. *Dan Kiley in His Own Words.* Thames and Hudson, London 1999

Levy, Leah. *Sculpting the Land* (Kathryn Gustafson). Spacemaker Press, Boston 1998

Owen, Jane. *Unearthing the Seeds of Chaos Theory.* (Charles Jencks' Garden of Cosmological Speculation in Scotland). *The Times Weekend*, London, 6 December 1997

Richardson, Tim. *How to Garden in a Jumping Universe* (Charles Jencks' Garden). *Country Life*, London, 23 October 1997

Smith, Ken. *Linear Landscapes.* Harvard Design Magazine, Spring 1999

Weilacher, Udo. *Between Landscape Architecture and Land Art.* Birkhauser Publishing, Basel/Berlin/Boston 1996

MATERIALS

Batstone, Karena and Helen Tindale. *Handbook for Garden Designers.* Ward Lock 1994

Black and Decker: *The Complete Guide to Decks.* Creative Publishing International. Minnetonka, Minnesota 1999

Conran, Sir Terence. *Garden DIY.* Conran Octopus, London 1991

Garnock, Jamie. *Trellis.* Thames and Hudson, London 1991

Gavin, Diarmuid. *Homefront in the Garden.* BBC, London 2001

Goldsworthy, Andy. *Stone.* Viking Press, London 1994

Goldsworthy, Andy. *Wall.* Thames and Hudson, London 2000

Guinness, Bunny. *Garden Workshop.* David and Charles, Devon 2001

Hessayon, D.G., Dr. *The Garden DIY Expert.* pbi Publishing, Waltham Cross 1992

Jacobsen, Arne. *St Catherine's College, Oxford.* wallpaper, London 1998

WATER

Archer-Wills, Anthony. *The Water Gardener.* Frances Lincoln, London 1993

Brookes, John. *Gardens of Paradise.* Weidenfeld and Nicolson, London 1987

Cooper, Guy and Gordon Taylor. *English Water Gardens.* Weidenfeld and Nicolson, London 1986

Jellicoe, Sir Geoffrey. *Shute House.* Academy Editions, London 1993

Keswick, Maggie. *The Chinese Garden.* Academy Editions, London 1986

Moore, Charles. *Water and Architecture.* Harry Abrams, New York 1995

Muhlberg, Helmut. *The Complete Guide to Water Plants* (trans: Ilse Lindsay). E.P. Publishing, London 1982

Nash, Helen and C. Greg Peichert. *Water Gardening in Containers.* Sterling Publishing, New York 1996

Paul, Anthony and Yvonne Rees. *The Water Garden.* Guide Publishing, London 1986

Perry, Frances. *Water Gardening. Country Life*, London 1938

Williams, Robin. *The Garden Planner.* Frances Lincoln, London 1990

SCULPTURE

Beardsley, John. *Gardens of Revelation.* Abbeville Publishing, New York 1995

Clarke, Ethne and George Wright. *English Topiary Gardens.* Weidenfeld and Nicolson, London 1988

Coleby, Nicola (Ed.). *A Surreal Life: Edward James.* The Royal Pavilion, Libraries and Museums, Brighton and Hove in association with Philip Watson Publishers, London 1998

Cooper, Guy and Gordon Taylor. *Gardens of Obsession.* Weidenfeld and Nicolson, London 1999

Gallup, Barbara and Deborah Reich. *The Complete Book of Topiary.* Workman Publishing Co., New York 1987

Mazzanti, Anna (Ed.). *Niki de Saint-Phalle – The Tarot Garden*. Edizioni Charta, Milan 1997

Mott, George. *Follies and Pleasure Pavilions*. Pavilion Books in association with The National Trust, London 1989

Owen, Jane. *Eccentric Gardens*. Weidenfeld and Nicolson, London 1990

Pliny the Elder. *The Natural History* (trans: J. Bostock and H.T. Riley). London 1855–7

Plumptre, George. *Garden Ornament*. Thames and Hudson, London 1989

Reames, Richard and Barbara Delbol. *How to Grow a Chair: The art of tree trunk topiary*. Arborsmith Studios, Oregon 1996

PLANTS

Abbott, Marylyn. *Gardens of Plenty: The art of the potager garden*. Kyle Cathie, London 2001

Adams, William Howard. *Roberto Burle Marx: The Unnatural Art of the Garden*. Museum of Modern Art, New York 1991

Bean, W.J. *Trees and Shrubs Hardy in the British Isles* (4 vols). John Murray, London 1970

Chatto, Beth. *The Dry Garden*. Orion, London 1998

Chatto, Beth. *The Damp Garden*. Orion, London 1998

Chatto, Beth. *Garden Notebook*. Orion, London 1998

Cooper, Guy and Gordon Taylor. *English Herb Gardens*. Weidenfeld and Nicolson, London 1985

Hay, Roy and Kenneth A. Beckett. *Reader's Digest Encyclopaedia of Garden Plants and Flowers*, London 1971

Jekyll, Gertrude. *Home and Garden*. Longmans, London 1900

Jekyll, Gertrude. *Roses for English Gardens*. Country Life, London 1902

Jekyll, Gertrude. *Colour Schemes for the Flower Garden*. Country Life, London 1908

Lloyd, Christopher. *The Adventurous Gardener*. Allen Lane, London 1983

Oehme and van Sweden. *Bold Romantic Gardens*. Acropolis Publishers, Virginia, USA 1990

Oudolf, Piet. *Designing with Plants*. Conran Octopus, London 1999

Pope, Nori and Sandra. *Colour by Design*. Conran Octopus, London 1998

Royal Horticultural Society Plant Finder (available annually)

Index

Pages referred to include
illustrations

A

Abbott, Marylyn 128–131
Ageratum 'Bluebird' 167
Aislabie, John 102–105
Aislabie, William 104–105
Alexander-Sinclair, James
    24–29
Alice in Wonderland models 129
aluminium cylinders 123
Alvescot (Shill House) 60–61
Ambassadors, The 117
amphitheatre 58–59
Anderson family 90–91
Anderton, Stephen 49, 65–67
Anglesey Abbey 13, 136–139
Antony 114–117
Archer-Wills, Anthony
    118–121
Aspinall, John 164–167

B

Baker, Sir Herbert 164, 166

Bampfylde, Copplestone Warre
    74
Banana plants 159, 170
Bartlett, Peter 152–155
Barton, Julia 18, 19, 34–37
Batstone, Karena 84–87
BBC team 5
Beaumont, Guillaume 34
berm 119
Beth Chatto Gardens, The 158,
    182–185
Birch trees 176
Blenheim Palace 101
Boscastle (Half Acre) 127,
    144–145
Bradley-Hole, Christopher
    66–67
Bridgeman, Charles 58–59
Brown, Lancelot ('Capability')
    19, 59
Bryant, Sir Arthur 137
Buckhurst Farm 152
Bude Light, The 145
Bunhill Fields 68
Burlington, Lord 66
Bury Court 179–181

C

Campbell, Colen 104, 105
Canas 159
Cardiff (Tindale & Batstone
    gardens) 85–87
Carew Pole family 114–117
Carter, George 132–135
Castle Cary (Hadspen Garden
    and Nursery) 12, 14, 158,
    160–163
cedar of Lebanon tree 81
Celtic necklace image 24
chadar 14, 15
change in gardens 10, 151
Chase, David 128
Chatto, Andrew 182
Chatto, Beth 158, 182–185
Checkerboard Garden 156, 164,
    167
Chinoiserie fruit cages 131
Chipping Campden
    (Hidcote Manor) 49, 54–57
chutes 15, 108–109,
circles and arcs 56, 60–61, 144,
    145, 151

Claremont Landscape Gardens
    11, 12, 58–59
Clive, Robert ('Clive of India') 59
Coke, John 179–181
Colchester (The Beth Chatto
    Gardens) 158, 182–185
Colour in the Flower Garden 22
concrete 70, 73, 84, 85, 89,
    126, 144
containers
    concrete 89
    copper 88–89
    galvanised 88
Conversation with Magic
    Stones 142, 143
Cook, Sarah 33
Cooper, Paul 38–39, 122–123
Coré 143
cottage garden 158
Cranbrook
    (Gardens of Gaia) 12, 13,
    127, 152–155
    (Sissinghurst Castle) 16, 19,
    30–33, 56, 127
Crawley (Maize maze) 19,
    40–42
Crowder, Chris 35

D

dahlia terrace 167
Dali, Salvador 150
deer park 105
Delaney, 'Topher 73
disposal of plants, brutal
    184–185
Dixon, Jeremy 110–113
Draughtsman's Contract, The 151
dry gardens 158, 184
Dudley family 44
Durngate (Anderson family,
    Flora's garden) 13, 90–91
Dutch influence 79, 127, 134

E

elements in gardens 11
Emperor's Walk 137
English Gardening School 84
Epping (floating gardens)
    122–123
Esher (Claremont Landscape
    Gardens) 11, 12, 58–59
Evelyn, John 134
evergreen plants 134–135, 145
Exotic Garden 159, 172–173,
    175

F

Fairhaven, Lord 136–139
Farnham (Bury Court) 179–181
Farrand, Beatrix 21
Farthing, Andrew 88
Fibonacci Sequence 145
fibre optic lighting 14, 73, 86,
    111 113
Findlay, Kathryn 92–95
Fisher, Adrian 19
Fitzroy, Yvonne 128
floating gardens 122–123
Flora's garden 13, 73, 90–91
Foley family 43
follies 50–53
form, effect on design 48
Fountains Abbey 102–105
fountains, largest in Europe 45
Four-square Walk Through 140,
    142
Framed Planting 168–169
Franklin, Alan 154
French influence 54, 133
furniture design 81

G

Garden in Mind 146–151

garden rooms and enclosures
    54, 61
Gardens of Gaia 12, 13, 127,
    152–155
Gavin, Diarmuid 90–91
geometric spaces 32
Getty Art Centre 154
gingko 142
Glasgow Garden Festival 26–28
glass technology 73
glasshouses
    twenty-first-century 12
    largest single span 49, 62–63
golden section 65–67
Gosport (Framed Planting)
    168–169
Great Dixter 13–14, 159,
    170–175
Great Plat 75–79
Great Witley (Witley Court)
    43–45
Green Room, The 38–39
Groombridge Place 151
Guardian of the Lake 155
Gustafson, Kathryn 49, 62–64,
    152

H

Hackney Community College
    96–97
Hadspen Garden and Nursery
    12, 14, 158, 160–163
Half Acre 127, 144–145
Hall, Henry 79
Hargreaves, George 152, 154
Hartley Wintney (West Green
    House) 128–131
Hatfield House 42
Hawksmoor 102
Hawkstone Inn 53
Hawkstone Park 48–49, 50–53
Hawley, General Henry 128
hedge maze 42
Hepworth, Dame Barbara 81,
    124, 127, 140–143, 144
herbaceous border 20, 158
Heron, Susanna 96–97
Hestercombe 13, 22, 73, 74–79
Het Loo 127
Hicks, Ivan 127, 146–151, 158,
    168–169
Hidcote Manor 49, 54–57
Hill, Sir Richard 49, 52
Hill, Sir Rowland 48–49, 50–53
Hobhouse, Penelope 21, 160
Holbein, Hans (the younger)
    117
hollyhocks 22

Holme, Charles 20, 23
hornbeam hedge 133, 134
Humpty Dumpty 154
Hythe (Port Lympne) 164–167

I

Impatiens 'Busy Lizzie' 167
influential garden 54
instant garden 38
Irwin, Robert 154
Isle of Bute (Mount Stuart) 12,
    19, 24–29
Italian influence 18, 19, 32, 54,
    97, 100–101, 127, 134

J

Jacobson, Arne 80–83
James, Edward 146
Jekyll, Gertrude
    Colour in the Flower Garden
        22
    Garden Ornament 99
    herbaceous borders 20, 158
    Hestercombe 22, 74–79
    Home and Garden 71
    Manor House, Upton Grey
        12, 18–19, 20–23
    modern design 71
    obituary 20
    plans 10, 12, 18–19, 21–23,
        78–79
    reflecting pool design 67
    Sutton Place 67
    water 99
    yucca 21
Jellicoe, Sir Geoffrey 67, 89, 101,
    106–109
Jenningsbury Farm 176–178
Jerwood Sculpture Park 43–45
Johnson, Dr Samuel 52
Johnston, Lawrence 49, 54–57
Jones, Alistair 88
Jones, Edward 110–113

K

Kendal (Levens Hall) 18, 19,
    34–37
Kennerton Green, New South
    Wales 129
Kent, William 59, 100, 102, 134
Kiley, Daniel 49, 99
Kirby, Rip 154
Kissing Archway 12, 154
Kreutzberger, Sibylle 33

L

labyrinths 40, 151
Landscapes Unlimited 88
lavender 22
Leonard Hotel, The 38–39
Levens Hall 18, 19, 34–37
Lewis family 109
Lexington, The 49, 68–69
leylandii hedging 151
light display 111–113
lighting in garden 123
Lime trees 161
Llewelyn-Bowen, Laurence 90
Lloyd Wright, Frank 48
Lloyd, Christopher 170–175
Lobelia 'Crystal Palace' 167
Lode (Anglesey Abbey) 13,
    136–139
London
    Hackney Community
        College 96–97
    Kennington ultra modern
        garden 88–89
    Leonard Hotel, The 38–39
    Lexington, The 49, 68–69
    Somerset House 101,
        110–113
    Tindale & Batstone garden 87
Long Border 175
Long Walk 57
Lutyens, Sir Edwin
    Gertrude Jekyll collaboration
        20
    Great Dixter 170
    Hestercombe 22, 73, 74–79
    New Delhi 164
    Trafalgar Square fountains
        111
Lyceum, The 49, 65–67

M

Magnolia grandiflora 141, 142
maintenance, simple 19
Maize mazes 19, 40–42
Mandalay bell 114–116
Mann, Thomas 128
Manor House, The, Upton Grey
    10, 12, 18–19, 20–23
Marinetti, Filippo 125
Marx, Roberto Burle 49, 68–69,
    157
mathematical maze 42
Mawson, Thomas 28–29
mazes 19, 40–42
McAlpine, Lord 128–129
Mediterranean plants 57, 62,
    63, 64, 79

Middleton Hall 62
Millets Farm 40
miscanthus 170
modernism 14, 65, 67
Monument, The 48, 50, 52
Moon Ponds 102, 103–105
Moore, Henry 143
Morte slate 73, 75, 78
Mount Stuart 12, 19, 24–29
municipal planting 168
Myers, Robert 68–69

N

Nash, John 43
nasturtium 33
National Botanic Garden of
    Wales 12, 49, 62–64, 152
National Trust 114, 117, 128
naturalistic lake 118–121
Nesfield, William 44–45
Newcastle, Duke of 58–59
Newport, Essex (The Lyceum)
    49, 65–67
Newton, Ernest 20
Nicholson, Ben 67, 140
Nicolson, Nigel 30, 32–33
Nicolson, Sir Harold 30–33, 56
North, Countess 28
nymphaeum 128

O

objets trouvés 127, 148–149, 151
octagonal pavilion 30
optical mazes 41–42
Oudolf, Piet 179–180
Owen, Jane 60–61
Oxford (St Catherine's College)
    80–83

P

Page, Russell 164–167
Palladio, Andrea 66
panoramic views 53, 55, 57, 165
Paradise Transformed;
    The Private Garden for the
    Twenty-First Century 85
Patel, Sal 15
patience needed in gardening
    19
Pavord, Anna 54
Paxton, Sir William 62
perennial borders and gardens
    18–19, 57, 158, 179–181
pergola columns 75
Phlox 'Violet Vere' 33
Phytoforms 18, 35

picture frames 168
picturesque walks 50–53
Playfair family 128
Pope, Sandra and Nori 12, 158,
    160–163
Porphyry bowl 136–137
Port Lympne 164–167
Portman, Hon Edward 74
Posas, Las, Mexico 146
potager 131
Pye, William 114–117

Q

quincunx 111

R

Rainier, Priaulx 140–143
Rambling Rector rose 134
re-creation of landscape 23
red hot pokers 22
Reef Point collection 21
reflecting pools 97
Rendell, Dominic 128
Repton, Humphry 114, 132
rills 13, 100, 108–109
Ring of Hope 154
Ripon (Fountains Abbey and
    Studley Royal) 13, 98,
    102–105
Robinson, William 158, 176
Rosa mulliganii 33
Rose, James C 47
Rothschild, Miriam 176
Rousham Park 100
Royal Botanic Gardens, Kew 24,
    28
Rye (Great Dixter) 13–14, 159,
    170–175

S

Sackville-West, Vita 30–33, 56
Safra, Mrs Lily 111
Salisbury, Lady 42
Sassoon, Sir Philip 164, 167
Schultz, Robert Weir 128
Schwerdt, Pam 33
sculptures 45, 60, 81, 96, 124,
    127, 140–143, 144
Shaftesbury (Shute House) 13,
    101, 106–109
shelter belt of trees 136
Shill House 60–61
Shute House 13, 101, 106–109
Silverstone Farm 132–135
Sissinghurst Castle 16, 19,
    30–33, 54, 56, 127

Sitwell, Sir George 17, 43
Skell, River 5, 104, 105
Smith, Eric 160
Smith, Sir Herbert 44
Soft and Hairy House 92–93
Somerset County Council 79
Somerset House 101, 110–113
St Catherine's College 80–83
St Ives (Trewyn Studio)
    140–143
stage in garden 66–67
Stanstead Park 146–151
Steele, Fletcher 14
Stoke, Ivor 64
Storrington (naturalistic lake)
    118–121
Stourhead 101
Striped Garden 164, 167
Studley Royal 13, 98, 102–105
Sunk Garden 175
Sutton Place 67
swimming pools
    first heated in Britain 28
    Thatched Pool House 93–95
Swiss bridge 51, 52

T

Tampa 40
Taunton (Hestercombe) 13, 22,
    73, 74–79
Terry, Quinlan 128
Thalictrum acquilegifolium
    'White Cloud' 33
Thatched Pool House 92–95
Theatre Lawn 56–57
Thomson, James 59
time in gardens 11, 19, 33
Tindale, Helen 84–87
Toll, Julie 176–178
Tolomei, Claudio 101
topiary 19, 34–37, 56, 114–116,
    127, 129, 175
Torpoint (Antony) 114–117
Trafalgar Square fountains 111
transitory nature of gardens 18
Trewyn Studio 140–143
Trojan steps 166
trompe l'oeil garden 135
Tsukuba New Science City
    92–93
Tulley's Farm 41
Tunnard, Christopher 10
Two forms (divided circle) 142

U

ultra modern garden 88–89

Upton Grey (The Manor House)
    10, 12, 18–19, 20–23
Ushida, Eisaku 92–95

V

Verbena 'Sissinghurst' 33
Verey, Rosemary 28–29
Versailles School of Landscape
    Architecture 154
viewing points 117
Villa Lante 100–101, 127
Villla d'Este 100
Vincent, Carole 127, 144–145

W

Wales, Augusta, Dowager
    Princess of 24–25
Wallinger, Rosamund 20–23
Water garden 184
water-earth junction 118
Wellington, Evelyn, Duchess of
    128
West Dean gardens 146
West Green House 128–131
Weston-under-Redcastle
    (Hawkstone Park) 50–53
White garden 33
wild flower meadow 176–178
Wilton House 101
Wines, James 92
Witley Court 43–45
Woodhams, Stephen 88–89

Y

yew walk 114
Yorke, Phillip 50
yucca 21